THE USER'S GUIDE TO

Women's Health Supplements

Learn What You Need to Know about Nutrients
and Herbs That Enhance Women's Health.

LAUREL VUKOVIC, MSW
Jack Challem Series Editor

Series Editor: Jack Challem
Editor: Roberta W. Waddell
Typesetter: Gary A. Rosenberg
Series Cover Designer: Mike Stromberg

Mondrose Press
Published by arrangement with Basic Health Publications, Inc.
8200 Boulevard East
North Bergen, NJ 07047
1-800-575-8890

Copyright © 2003 by Laurel Vukovic, MSW

ISBN: 1-59120-082-2

Printed in the United States of America

10   9   8   7   6   5   4   3   2   1

CONTENTS

INTRODUCTION

Women are different from men in more ways than meet the eye. The most fundamental difference can probably be summed up in one word: hormones. The same hormones that give a woman her feminine characteristics and enable her to create a child are also the cause of many of the health problems that are unique to women.

From the time a young girl's body begins to prepare for menstruation, through pregnancy, menopause, and the years beyond, a woman's body and emotions are influenced by her shifting hormones. Women have special needs to consider, needs that have not always been taken into account by conventional medicine and researchers. It's only in recent years that researchers have started realizing that, although men and women share some physiological traits, women are different, and need to be treated as such.

For example, although drinking alcohol may have some positive health benefits, such as lowering cholesterol levels, it also appears to increase a woman's risk of breast cancer. And while, for many years, women were thought to be virtually exempt from cardiovascular disease, it's now clear that women, after menopause, have an equal, and possibly greater, risk of heart disease than men.

There is still a great deal to learn about women's health, and researchers are attempting at this moment to find the keys to PMS, menopause, osteoporosis, breast cancer, and heart disease. Information revealing the latest findings about women's health appears almost daily in newspapers and magazines, and much of it can be confusing and even contradictory.

What we do know for certain is that diet and lifestyle play a central role in health. It's never too early to begin to eat well, exercise, and adopt healthful habits that will help prevent degenerative diseases such as cancer, heart disease, and osteoporosis. In fact, research shows that risk factors for these diseases begin as early as the teen years, because lifestyle habits have a cumulative effect. However, no matter what your current age or level of health, it's never too late to upgrade your diet and lifestyle to enhance your well-being.

By reading this book, you're taking a significant step toward improving your health and well-being. Perhaps you're suffering from one of the common ailments that affect women, such as menstrual cramps or PMS. If you're pregnant, you might be looking for information about how you can best care for yourself and your baby. Or you may be entering menopause, and wondering how you can smoothly navigate this significant life transition.

In the pages ahead, you'll discover clear and concise information that will help you to be as healthy as possible at every stage of life. You'll find specific recommendations for common problems associated with menstruation, suggestions for a healthy pregnancy, and guidance for the menopausal years. You'll also find comprehensive information about how you can avoid cancer, heart disease, and osteoporosis. The last chapter will help you choose, and get the most out of, dietary supplements.

Read through this book from start to finish if you want an overall guide to health care throughout a woman's life. If you have a particular health concern, turn right to that particular chapter. By following the suggestions you find in these pages, you can begin today to improve your health.

CHAPTER 1

MENSTRUATION AND MENSTRUAL DIFFICULTIES

The onset of menstruation is a significant physiological and emotional event in a young girl's life, and will likely be a monthly occurrence for approximately forty years. The subtle but powerful hormonal shifts that regulate the menstrual cycle can cause a variety of problems, ranging from cramps to endometriosis. In this chapter, you'll learn the most important factors for supporting healthy reproductive function, and you'll discover natural remedies for relieving common problems associated with menstruation.

The Basics of Menstruation

In the United States, most girls generally begin menstruating at about the age of twelve. But it's also perfectly normal if a girl begins to menstruate as early as age ten, or as late as age seventeen. The onset of menstruation seems to be dependent upon a girl having a sufficient amount of body fat, which is related to estrogen production. Girls who exercise regularly and strenuously, such as athletes or dancers, may begin menstruating later, as may those who diet excessively.

Each month, beginning at puberty, a woman's body prepares for possible pregnancy. The female reproductive organs consist of the ovaries, fallopian tubes, and uterus. The fallopian tubes connect the ovaries to the uterus, and are the channel through which eggs stored in the ovaries travel to the uterus. At birth, an infant girl's ovaries hold the thousands of eggs that will be released during her fertile years.

In the first phase of the menstrual cycle, the endometrium, or lining of the uterus, builds up layers of extra blood and tissue. Midway through the cycle, a ripened egg is released from an ovary. The egg passes through the fallopian tube, and if it is fertilized by sperm, the egg attaches to the wall of the thickened uterus, where it begins the process of developing into a baby. Most of the time, however, the egg

> **Endometrium**
> *The lining of the uterus, which builds up extra layers of tissue in the first phase of the menstrual cycle.*

is not fertilized and it simply dissolves. The extra blood and tissue built up by the uterus is shed and leaves the body through the vagina. This process continues each month until pregnancy occurs, or until ovulation ceases at menopause.

The average menstrual cycle is generally about twenty-eight days, but some women menstruate every twenty-one days, and some menstruate every forty-five days. The average menstrual period lasts from three to five days, but anywhere from two to seven days is also considered normal. The amount of bleeding during menstruation varies between women, too, and is the result of how much blood and tissue have been built up in the uterus. The menstrual cycle is controlled by the hormonal interplay of the hypothalamus, the pituitary gland, and the ovaries, which produce the primary female hormones, estrogen and progesterone. Estrogen governs the first half of the menstrual cycle; following ovulation, estrogen levels subside and progesterone levels increase.

A woman's menstrual cycle is governed by this intricate dance of hormones, and hormonal production is significantly affected by diet, emotions, and lifestyle. Let's look at some of the most common problems related to the menstrual cycle.

Menstrual Cramps

More than half of all women experience menstrual cramps (medically known as dysmenorrhea) to some degree. Cramping generally occurs in the pelvic area, but it's also common for the pain to radiate into the lower back and down

> **Dysmenorrhea**
> *The medical term for menstrual cramps, which most commonly occur in the pelvic area and affect more than half of all women.*

into the legs. For some women, cramps merely cause

mild discomfort, but for others, menstrual cramps can be painfully severe and incapacitating. Severe menstrual cramps often cause associated symptoms, such as diarrhea, low-back pain, and nausea.

The Cause of Cramps

Although menstrual cramps can be caused by a medical problem, such as endometriosis, a pelvic infection, or uterine fibroids, in the vast majority of cases, cramps are not the result of any physiological disorder. Cramps are often simply the result of the uterus working to expel menstrual blood and tissue. Hormonelike substances called series-2 prostaglandins can also trigger cramps. These inflammatory substances constrict blood vessels, inhibiting the flow of blood to the uterus and causing cramping. Blood-calcium levels also usually fall just prior to menstruation, and low levels of calcium can contribute to cramps, as can hypothyroidism (an underactive thyroid).

While series-2 prostaglandins are prime troublemakers in menstrual cramps, another type—called series-1 prostaglandins—has beneficial pain-relieving and hormone-balancing benefits.

Series-1 prostaglandins are made from linolenic acid (omega-3 fatty acids) and series-2 prostaglandins are derived from linoleic acid (omega-6 fatty acids). What you eat has a direct effect on which type of prostaglandins are dominant in your body. Omega-3 fatty acids are found in cold-water fish, such as mackerel, salmon, and sardines, and in flaxseeds and walnuts. Omega-6 fatty acids are found in grains, meats, seeds, and vegetable oils. Because omega-6 fatty acids are so abundant in the typical diet and omega-3 fatty acids are so scarce, most women get far more linoleic acid than linolenic acid. To add to the

> **Prostaglandins**
> *Hormonelike substances. Some have beneficial pain-relieving effects, others have inflammatory properties that can trigger cramps.*

problem, hydrogenated oils and the foods containing them (such as most chips, cookies, crackers, and processed foods) also stimulate the production of inflammatory series-2 prostaglandins. It's easy to understand how an excess of series-2 prostaglandins can arise.

Strategies for Easing Cramps

To increase the levels of series-1 prostaglandins, eat foods that are good sources of omega-3 fatty acids frequently. Try to eat at least two servings of cold-water fish per week, as well as a small handful of raw walnuts, or a tablespoon of freshly ground flaxseed several times a week. You might also consider supplementing your diet with one tablespoon of cold-pressed flaxseed oil daily. Taking supplements of gamma-linolenic acid (GLA), another essential fatty acid, can also help to balance prostaglandin production. GLA is found in black currant oil, borage oil, and evening primrose oil. Take enough capsules to equal 240 mg of GLA daily.

Eating foods rich in calcium and magnesium is another dietary strategy for helping to prevent menstrual cramps. Both of these essential minerals have a natural relaxing effect on the body. Dark leafy greens, legumes, nuts, and seeds are good sources of both calcium and magnesium. Taking a daily supplement of 1,000 mg of calcium and 400 mg of magnesium will boost your intake into an optimal range.

Regular exercise—at least thirty minutes five times a week—will also help to relieve menstrual cramps. Both aerobic exercise, such as brisk walking, and stretching exercises, such as yoga, increase circulation to the pelvic organs and help to relieve the emotional and physical tension that exacerbates menstrual cramps.

An excellent herbal remedy for easing menstrual cramps is cramp bark (*Viburnum opulus*). It contains natural compounds that help to relax the uterus. Take one-half to one teaspoon of liquid extract, or two capsules three to four times daily, as needed.

Sometimes, the simplest remedy can provide immediate relief from cramping. Give yourself some time out from your daily activities, and rest with your feet up and a hot water bottle over your abdomen for at least half an hour.

Supplements for Relieving Menstrual Cramps

- Calcium: 1,000 mg daily

- Magnesium: 400 mg daily

- Flaxseed oil: 1 tablespoon daily

- GLA: 240 mg daily

- Cramp bark (as needed): $1/2$ to 1 teaspoon liquid extract or 2 capsules three to four times daily

Premenstrual Syndrome

During their reproductive years, most women will experience, to at least some degree, premenstrual syndrome (PMS). Abdominal bloating, backache, breast tenderness, digestive disturbances, fatigue, headache, insomnia, joint pain, mood swings, and water retention are just some of the many ways that shifts in hormones affect a woman's body and mind.

The Causes of PMS

PMS most commonly occurs during the week to ten days prior to the onset of menstruation. Some women, however, are plagued by PMS symptoms throughout most of the month.

Although the precise cause of PMS has not been determined, PMS symptoms appear to be caused by an excess of estrogen in relation to progesterone, and by increased levels of the inflammatory series-2 prostaglandins. Symptoms may also be related to the dip in calcium and magnesium levels that occurs prior to menstruation. For some women, premenstrual symptoms are mild and insignificant. For others, however, PMS can be debilitating, both physically and emotionally. While there is still much to learn about PMS, it is clear that diet and exercise play an important role in the onset and severity of symptoms.

The Role of Diet in PMS

What you eat on a daily basis determines how well your body processes hormones. Through your dietary choices, you can help your body eliminate excess estrogen, reduce problem-causing prostaglandins while enhancing the production of beneficial prostaglandins, and improve hormonal balance.

A high-fiber diet that is rich in fruits, vegetables, legumes, and whole grains, helps your body eliminate excess estrogen. Nurturing a healthy population of intestinal flora also aids the intestinal tract in its job of excreting estrogen, and a diet rich in complex carbohydrates, such as fruits, vegetables, and whole grains, encourages the growth of these beneficial flora. To replenish healthy bacteria in the intestinal tract, you can also take supplements of probiotic bacteria such as *Lactobacillus*

Probiotic Bacteria
Beneficial bacteria, such as lactobacillus acidophilus and bifidobacterium bifidum, that aid in digestion and elimination and help to keep the intestinal tract healthy.

acidophilus and *Bifidobacterium bifidum*. Take a supplement that supplies at least five billion live bacteria daily.

Curtailing your intake of hydrogenated and partially hydrogenated fats, polyunsaturated vegetable oils, and saturated fat also helps to lower estrogen levels and decreases the production of inflammatory prostaglandins. As much as possible, don't eat meat or dairy foods that have been produced with hormones, and avoid toxins, such as pesticides and fungicides, which have estrogenic activity.

If you suffer from PMS, it's best to stay away from all sources of caffeine, including coffee, tea, chocolate, and caffeinated soft drinks. Even the small amounts of caffeine found in decaffeinated coffee or tea can trigger PMS symptoms. To prevent mood and energy swings, eat small, frequent meals that are high in protein and low in sugar.

To improve hormonal balance and encourage the production of beneficial prostaglandins, eat foods rich in omega-3 fatty acids, such as salmon, sardines, walnuts, and flaxseed oil. Aim for three servings of fish per week, and a small handful of walnuts or one tablespoon of ground flaxseeds or flaxseed oil daily. In addition, take 240 mg daily of gamma-linolenic acid (GLA), found in black currant, borage seed, and evening primrose oils.

Soy foods, such as soy milk, tempeh, and tofu, are excellent sources of plant estrogens, which also help to regulate estrogen levels. Consume one serving of soy daily: four ounces of tempeh or tofu, or one cup of soy milk.

Supplements for PMS

To help your body metabolize estrogen more efficiently, take a high-potency B-complex vitamin daily. Vitamin B_6 is particularly important here because it supports the liver in its job of breaking down estrogen, and also helps to alleviate premenstrual bloating and mood swings.

In addition, you can support optimal liver function (the liver plays a critical role in metabolizing and detoxifying estrogen) by taking a supplement that contains the lipotropic agents choline, methionine and/or cysteine. Take 1,000 mg of choline and 500 mg of methionine or cysteine every day.

> **Lipotropic Agents**
> *Nutrients that enhance the liver's function of metabolizing and detoxifying estrogen by improving fat metabolism and promoting bile flow.*

Other useful supplements include calcium and magnesium. A recent study of 466 women at St. Luke's-Roosevelt Hospital in New York showed that calcium supplements effectively relieve PMS symptoms such as mood swings, pain, and water retention. The women, aged eighteen to forty-five, were randomly divided into two groups. Half were given 1,200 mg of calcium daily, and the rest were given a placebo. After three months, those taking the calcium supplement reported a 48 percent reduction in symptoms, compared with those in the control group who reported only a 30 percent reduction in symptoms.

Magnesium is necessary for your liver to metabolize estrogen, and it's also needed to stabilize blood sugar levels. In addition, low levels of magnesium contribute to fluid retention. If you have a strong craving for chocolate premenstrually, it may be your body telling you that you need magnesium. Chocolate is rich in magnesium, but it's not the best way to get this nutrient because the caffeine and sugar in chocolate tend to make PMS symptoms worse. Instead, try eating magnesium-rich foods, such as legumes, nuts, and seeds, and take 400–600 mg of magnesium daily.

Vitamin E is important for relieving breast tenderness, which is a common symptom associated with PMS. Take 400–800 IU of vitamin E daily.

In addition to a healthful diet and supplements, exercise is essential for relieving PMS. Regular exercise, at least thirty minutes a day, helps regulate hormone levels and stimulates the production of endorphins, the body's natural mood-elevating chemicals. In addition, exercise helps to ease the emotional tension that is often a component of PMS.

> **Endorphins**
> *The body's natural mood-elevating chemicals. They can be increased by exercising.*

Herbal Help for PMS

Herbs can help regulate hormonal balance and can also ease the symptoms of PMS. Perhaps the most important is chasteberry (*Vitex agnus-castus*), which has been used since the time of Hippocrates to tone and regulate the reproductive system. Chasteberry improves the functioning of the pituitary gland, which is responsible for regulating the production of progesterone. By increasing the production of progesterone, chasteberry helps to bring hormones into a more favorable balance.

In a 1994 German study of 550 women with PMS and menstrual disorders, 32 percent of the participants showed improvement within the first four weeks after taking chasteberry. By the end of the third menstrual cycle, 84 percent of the women demonstrated an improvement in their symptoms. For best results, chasteberry should be taken over a long period of time—at least six months. Take one-half teaspoon of liquid extract, or one capsule up to three times a day.

St. John's wort (*Hypericum perforatum*) is helpful for the depression, insomnia, irritability, and mood swings that commonly occur in PMS.

A study of nineteen women at the University of Exeter in

> **Lactobacillus Acidophilus and Bifidobacterium Bifidum**
> *Beneficial flora, called probiotics, that are found in the intestinal tract and aid in digestion and assimilation.*

the United Kingdom showed that two-thirds of these women found significant relief when taking St. John's wort. They were given 900 mg of the herb daily for two complete menstrual cycles, and reported that their PMS-related symptoms of anxiety, confusion, crying, depression, and nervous tension were diminished by more than half.

Supplements for PMS

- Calcium: 1,000 mg daily

- Magnesium: 400–600 mg daily

- Vitamin-B complex: 50–100 mg daily

- Vitamin E: 400–800 IU daily

- Flaxseed oil: 1 tablespoon daily

- GLA (black currant seed, borage seed, or evening primrose oil): 240 mg daily

- Lipotrophic formula: 1,000 mg choline and 500 mg methionine and/or cysteine daily

- Probiotic formula: 5–10 billion viable *Lactobacillus acidophilus* and *Bifidobacterium bifidum* daily

- Chasteberry: 1/2 teaspoon liquid extract or one 500– 600 mg capsule one to three times daily

- St. John's wort (as needed): 300 mg three times daily

Cervical Dysplasia

Cervical dysplasia is the medical term that is used to describe abnormal cell growth in the cervix, which is the entrance to the uterus. Although cervical dysplasia is considered to be a precancerous condition, it is easily treatable and reversible when it is discovered early.

Understanding Cervical Dysplasia

Abnormal cell growth is diagnosed through a Pap smear, which is a routine gynecological exam. Cells taken from the cervix are examined and graded on a scale of one to four, with higher numbers indicating greater cell abnormality. If you have stage-2 dysplasia, your doctor will probably simply want to monitor your condition. Many times, stage-2 dysplasia heals with no need for medical intervention. If you have stage-3 or stage-4 dysplasia, you should be treated by a physician. In any case, you can use the information in this section to reduce your risk of further cell abnormalities.

Risk factors for cervical dysplasia include birth control pills, cigarette smoking, exposure to the genital herpes virus or venereal warts, multiple sexual partners, and sexual activity before the age of eighteen. In addition, cervical dysplasia has been strongly linked to an insufficient intake of the B-complex vitamins, especially folic acid.

If you have been diagnosed with cervical dysplasia, it is important to rule out a vaginal infection, which could be the underlying reason for cell abnormalities. If a vaginal infection is the cause, treating it will resolve the condition.

Dietary Factors in Cervical Dysplasia

The incidence of cervical dysplasia and cervical cancer is clearly associated with deficiencies of a variety of nutrients. Studies of women suffering from cervical dysplasia show that they have insufficient blood levels of antioxidants and folic acid.

Folic acid, a B-complex vitamin, is especially important for preventing and reversing cervical dysplasia. Dark leafy greens are an excellent source of this nutrient. Eat at least one generous serving of collards, kale, spinach, or other dark leafy greens daily. In addition, take a B-complex supplement that contains 400 mcg of folic acid. If you have been diagnosed with cervical dysplasia, take 10 mg of folic acid daily for up to three months, along with a high-potency B-complex supplement.

If you have cervical dysplasia, eating a diet rich in fresh fruits and vegetables, and supplementing with antioxidants is essential for protecting cells and preventing abnormal cell growth. As a general daily antioxidant supplement, take 25,000 IU of beta-carotene with mixed carotenoids, 500 mg of vitamin C, 200 mcg of selenium, and 400 IU of vitamin E.

Supplements for Cervical Dysplasia

- B-complex: 50–100 mg daily

- Folic acid: 400 mcg daily; 10 mg daily for three months if cervical dysplasia is present
- Beta-carotene: 25,000 IU with mixed carotenoids
- Selenium: 200 mcg daily
- Vitamin C: 500 mg daily
- Vitamin E: 400 IU daily

Uterine Fibroids

Almost half of all women develop uterine fibroids, a benign growth of muscle tissue in the uterus. Fibroids can be as tiny as the head of a pin, or as large as a grapefruit, and it's not uncommon for a woman to have multiple fibroid growths in her uterus.

Understanding Uterine Fibroids

Although fibroids often present no symptoms, they can cause heavy menstrual bleeding, irregular menstrual periods, and pelvic discomfort. Fibroids are not associated with a higher incidence of uterine cancer, but they are one of the primary reasons for hysterectomies. Many times, a woman can live with fibroids for years without problems. However, the fluctuating hormones that occur during the perimenopausal years often trigger the increased growth of existing fibroids, and can exacerbate their symptoms.

> **Perimenopause**
> *The months or years of hormonal fluctuations prior to menopause.*

More serious symptoms of fibroids include anemia

brought on by heavy menstrual bleeding, or discomfort of the bladder or bowel if the fibroid puts pressure on the bladder or intestines. Unless a fibroid growth is causing undue discomfort, or becomes a health risk, it's safe to simply leave it alone. In the vast majority of cases, fibroids shrink dramatically after menopause. Meanwhile, there are ways you can ease your symptoms and perhaps even reduce the size of your fibroids.

Dietary Help for Fibroids

If you have been diagnosed with fibroids, the most important thing you can do is decrease your body's production of estrogen. Avoid all animal products (such as dairy products, eggs, poultry, and meat) that have been grown or treated with hormones or drugs. Also stay away from foods treated with herbicides and pesticides because these substances have hormonal effects in the body. Hydrogenated fats and saturated fats also stimulate the production of estrogen.

A fiber-rich diet will help your body eliminate excess estrogen. Fresh fruits and vegetables, legumes, and whole grains are excellent sources of dietary fiber. Include soy products such as tempeh and tofu in your diet as often as possible—every day, if you can. Soy helps to naturally regulate estrogen levels.

In addition to dietary changes, daily aerobic exercise, such as bicycling or brisk walking, is essential for bringing hormones into balance.

Natural Therapies for Fibroids

To help your body metabolize estrogen more efficiently, take a high-potency B-complex vitamin daily. In addition, you can help your liver function at its best (the liver plays a critical role in metabolizing and detoxifying estrogen) by taking a supplement that contains the lipotropic agents choline, methionine and/or cysteine. Take 1,000 mg of choline and 500 mg of methionine or cysteine daily.

Nurturing a healthy population of intestinal flora also helps the body to eliminate excess estrogen. A diet rich in complex carbohydrates, such as fruits, vegetables, and whole grains, helps to feed beneficial flora, and supplements of probiotic bacteria such as *Lactobacillus acidophilus* and *Bifidobacterium bifidum* replenish healthy bacteria in the intestinal tract. Take a supplement that supplies at least five billion live bacteria daily.

An herb that can help to reduce fibroid growth is chasteberry. It stimulates the production of progesterone, which creates a more favorable balance of hormones and lessens the effect of estrogen on the body. For best results, take chasteberry for at least six months. Take one-half teaspoon of liquid extract or one capsule three times daily.

Supplements for Uterine Fibroids

- B-complex: 50–100 mg daily

- Chasteberry: ½ teaspoon liquid extract or one 500–600 mg capsule three times daily

- Lipotrophic formula: 1,000 mg choline and 500 mg methionine and/or cysteine daily

- Probiotic formula: 5–10 billion viable *Lactobacillus acidophilus* and *Bifidobacterium bifidum* daily

CHAPTER 2

PREGNANCY AND BIRTH

Pregnancy and birth are generally wonderful events in a woman's life. At the same time, pregnancy brings challenges as a woman's body undergoes the task of creating a life and preparing for birth. In this chapter, you'll learn about diet, supplements, and lifestyle factors that will keep you and your growing baby healthy. You'll also find suggestions for the common problems that plague pregnant women, such as morning sickness and constipation.

Preparing for Pregnancy

Paying attention to your health is always important, but it's doubly so when you're pregnant. If you're of childbearing age and considering having a child, it's best to plan ahead for a healthy pregnancy. During your nine months of pregnancy, your body will go through many changes as the baby develops. Pregnancy places great demands on a woman's body, and your baby is completely dependent upon you to provide what it needs to grow healthy and strong.

The first trimester is the most critical stage in your baby's development, because this is the time that major organs are being formed. Your nutritional needs during pregnancy are different than usual, and it's necessary to pay close attention to your diet to make sure you are supplying your baby with everything it needs. A healthy diet is also vital for your well-being, because the baby draws nutrients from you and can leave you depleted if your diet is inadequate. In addition to providing all the necessary nutrients for your baby, it's essential to avoid all substances that can harm your baby, such as alcohol, drugs (other than those prescribed by your doctor), and smoking.

During the first three months, many women experience uncomfortable symptoms such as fatigue, mood swings, and nausea. In later stages of pregnancy, as the baby grows larger, you may suffer from backaches, constipation, difficulties sleeping, and needing to go to the bathroom frequently. Although unpleasant, it can be helpful to know that these discomforts are normal, and are related to shifting hormones and your body's adjusting to the growing baby. It's important to listen to your body, to give yourself time to rest, and to nurture yourself as much as possible.

Throughout your pregnancy, you should stay in close touch with your healthcare practitioner, who can offer guidance for your particular needs.

A Healthy Diet for Pregnancy

What you eat during pregnancy is vital for your health and the well-being of your baby. Your diet should be centered on nutrient-dense foods such as fresh fruits and vegetables, high-quality proteins, and whole grains. You should figure on gaining about twenty-five to thirty-five extra pounds during pregnancy. While you don't want to pile on unnecessary pounds, pregnancy is not the time to diet.

Certain nutrients, particularly calcium, folic acid, and iron, are especially essential during pregnancy. Folic acid, a member of the B-complex vitamin family, is required for the formation of a healthy brain and spinal cord. A deficiency of this nutrient during pregnancy has been clearly linked to two serious birth defects: spina bifida, a defect of the spinal column that can cause paralysis and mental retardation, and anencephaly, a defect where the baby does not develop a brain and is stillborn or dies shortly after birth.

Folic acid is found abundantly in dark leafy green vegetables, dried beans, peas, and citrus fruits, but few women get enough from dietary sources. Taking a supplement that provides 400 mcg of folic acid is critical for protecting your baby. Because the fetus needs folic acid within the first few weeks of development, you should be taking supplements of folic acid all the time, not just while you're pregnant. Folic acid has many other health benefits as well, such as preventing cervical-cell abnormalities, so it's a good idea to take it regularly throughout your life, anyway.

Iron is also necessary for you and your baby, and ensures the production of healthy, oxygen-carrying red blood cells. A deficiency of iron causes anemia, a frequent reason for excessive fatigue during pregnancy. Anemia can increase a pregnant woman's susceptibility to infections, and make it more difficult for her body to cope with excessive bleeding during childbirth.

Many foods are high in iron, including dark green leafy vegetables, dried beans, dried fruits, nuts, seeds, chicken, salmon, shellfish, and red meat. But iron is not easily assimilated. And some foods, especially caffeine, milk, and bran, inhibit iron absorption. You can enhance iron's absorption by eating foods high in vitamin C at the same time that you eat iron-rich foods. Because getting enough iron is tricky, and low iron levels are so common among pregnant women, most women need supplements of it during pregnancy. Your doctor can perform a simple blood test and will tell you if you need supplemental iron.

Adequate calcium intake is essential for a woman throughout her life, and pregnancy is no exception. During pregnancy, the baby needs calcium for making bones and teeth. If your calcium intake is less than optimal, the baby will draw on the calcium stored in your bones, leaving you at risk for osteoporosis later in life. During pregnancy, you need to consume enough calcium for both you and your baby. The recommended amount of calcium for a pregnant woman is 1,200 mg per day.

Many foods are good sources of calcium, including cheeses, milk, yogurt, and dark leafy greens. Milk and yogurt contain about 300 mg of calcium per cup, so four one-cup servings per day will provide you with your ration of calcium. But many women either don't like milk or don't digest it easily. Alternative sources of calcium include dark leafy greens, with one cup of cooked collards weighing in at 300 mg of calcium and one cup of cooked kale at 200 mg. However, it's unlikely that you'll eat four to six cups of cooked greens. To obtain sufficient calcium, you may need calcium supplements. It's best to consult your health practitioner for advice.

Be sure to eat a wide variety of fresh vegetables and fruits while you're pregnant. They are excellent sources of protective antioxidants, especially dark green leafy vegetables and deep yellow and orange fruits and vegetables. A number of studies have linked insufficient intake of antioxidants to preeclampsia, a serious condition that causes fluid retention, headaches, and high blood pressure. If preeclampsia is not treated, it can progress to eclampsia, which can result in convulsions, coma, and death. This is another good reason to take a well-balanced prenatal multivitamin and mineral during pregnancy.

Fluid intake is also important while you are pregnant, because your blood volume greatly increases to accommodate your growing baby. Keeping your fluid intake up can also help ward off constipation. Drink at least eight glasses of water daily.

Other Lifestyle Suggestions for Pregnancy

While you are pregnant, it's essential that you completely avoid alcoholic beverages, including wine and beer. Drinking alcohol can cause fetal alcohol syndrome, a significant and completely preventable cause of birth defects and mental retardation. You should also avoid or limit your consumption of caffeine, which can cause insomnia, nervousness, and dehydration. Excessive amounts of caffeine may also result in low-birth-weight babies. Coffee is not the only offender: tea, cola, chocolate, cocoa, and some over-the-counter drugs, including pain relievers and allergy medicines, are also significant sources of caffeine.

If you smoke, you must stop, not only for your own health, but also for the health of your baby. Smoking puts your baby at risk for a low birth weight, and smokers are in danger of having premature or still-born babies. Babies born to mothers who smoke during pregnancy are more susceptible to asthma and respiratory infections, and are at higher risk of sudden infant death syndrome (SIDS). Because breathing second-hand smoke is also unhealthy, you should avoid being around people who smoke.

While you are pregnant, you should also avoid x-rays, which expose the baby to radiation and can cause birth defects. And hot tubs and saunas are not appropriate during pregnancy because they can raise core body temperature, which may harm the developing baby. Soaking in a warm bath is fine, though, and can be wonderfully relaxing. Just make sure that the temperature is not excessively hot.

Exercise is an indispensable ingredient for optimal well-being, and pregnancy is no exception. A 1998 study published in the *American Journal of Public Health* reported that women who engaged in regular, vigorous exercise were more likely to carry their babies to full term than those who didn't exercise, or who exercised less. Exercise maintains muscle and cardiovascular fitness, improves sleep, relieves tension, and enhances mood. Obviously, you shouldn't participate in contact sports or those that involve a risk of falling, such as downhill skiing.

The best exercises during pregnancy are brisk walking, prenatal aerobics classes, riding a stationary bicycle, and swimming. Prenatal yoga classes are excellent for stretching and relaxation. Exercise is appropriate for the majority of pregnant women, but you should check with your healthcare practitioner before starting an exercise program.

Common Problems during Pregnancy

Pregnancy is often fraught with minor, but annoying

maladies, such as morning sickness, constipation, and frequent urination. Morning sickness is somewhat of a misnomer, because nausea and vomiting can occur at any time during the day. Nausea plagues the majority of women during the first trimester, and, for some women, it persists throughout the entire nine months. The hormonal changes of pregnancy are a likely cause of morning sickness, but recent theories also suggest that nausea is your body's way of protecting your baby from foods that may be harmful.

To ease symptoms of nausea, pay attention to what your body is telling you. Don't eat foods that you find unappealing, or that upset your stomach. You'll probably find that your tastes change during pregnancy, and the best thing to do is to follow your intuition. You may find it helpful to eat frequent, smaller meals and drink less fluid with meals. Many women also find that starchy carbohydrates, such as crackers, help to ease nausea.

Ginger (*Zingiber officinale*) has been proven in numerous research studies to effectively relieve nausea, and it's safe to use during pregnancy. In a study reported in the *European Journal of Obstetrics & Gynecology*, ginger was shown to be more effective than a placebo for easing the nausea and vomiting of severe morning sickness. Drink up to three cups of ginger tea daily (it's best to sip $\frac{1}{4}$ to $\frac{1}{2}$ cup of tea at a time) or take up to 250 mg in capsules up to four times a day.

Almost half of all pregnant women suffer from constipation. Hormonal changes relax the muscle tone of the large intestine, which slows the passage of food through the digestive tract. Iron supplements, which are commonly prescribed to treat anemia, can also be the culprit. Drinking plenty of water, eating a fiber-rich diet, and exercising daily are often enough to cure constipation. A daily ration of stewed prunes is another time-honored way of encouraging sluggish bowels to move.

For extra help, you can take a fiber supplement, such as those made from psyllium, to provide additional bulk. Be sure to drink plenty of additional water when taking a fiber supplement to avoid creating constipation. During pregnancy, you should never resort to stimulant laxatives (such as those made from senna or cascara sagrada) because of the risk of causing uterine contractions.

While your intestines may be slowing down during pregnancy, your kidneys and bladder are doing the opposite, and you will probably experience an increased need to urinate, even when your bladder is almost empty. During pregnancy, your kidneys step up their activity, and as the baby grows, it puts pressure on your bladder. It's important to urinate as often as you feel the need, and to keep drinking plenty of fluids—at least eight glasses of water daily—to prevent bladder infections. If you have pain, burning, or difficulty urinating, consult your health practitioner right away. An untreated bladder infection can spread to the kidneys and be life-threatening.

To help prevent bladder infections, drink sixteen ounces of unsweetened cranberry juice daily. Cranberry juice helps to foil infection by making the walls of the bladder slippery, which keeps bacteria from attaching to the bladder walls and multiplying. You can also take capsules of cranberry extract; follow the directions on the label.

If you come down with any kind of infection during pregnancy, echinacea (*Echinacea spp.*) is an excellent herb to help support your immune function. Echinacea is effective for treating bladder infections, colds and respiratory infections, sinus infections, and other common illnesses. A recent study reported in the *Archives of Internal Medicine* showed that echinacea is safe during pregnancy. In general, take one-half teaspoon of echinacea extract four times a day for up to ten days. If you contract any type of infection during pregnancy, consult your healthcare practitioner for advice.

Supplements for Pregnancy

Consult your doctor before taking any supplements during pregnancy.

A prenatal multivitamin and mineral daily, which should contain:

• Antioxidants: (beta-carotene and mixed carotenoids, vitamin E, vitamin C)

- Calcium: 1,200 mg daily (less if dietary sources are sufficient)

- Folic acid: 400 mcg daily

- Iron: 15–30 mg daily

For morning sickness:

- Ginger: three cups of tea; or 250 mg in capsules up to four times daily

For constipation:

- Fiber supplement: 1–3 tablespoons daily

For colds and other infections:

- Echinacea: $\frac{1}{2}$ teaspoon extract four times daily for up to ten days

CHAPTER 3

MENOPAUSE

The menopausal years are a time of great change for a woman, and affect all levels of her physical and emotional well-being. Most women experience at least some of the symptoms that are commonly associated with menopause, such as forgetfulness, heart palpitations, hot flashes, joint pain, mood swings, sleep disturbances, urinary tract infections, and vaginal dryness. At this time in life, it becomes more important than ever before to pay attention to your health.

The Challenges of Menopause

The hormonal changes that a woman experiences in the years surrounding menopause are powerful. The conventional medical approach to menopause is to prescribe hormone therapy (HRT), both for symptom relief and for preventing cardiovascular disease and osteoporosis in postmenopausal women. The combination of estrogen and progesterone is often effective for relieving depression, hot flashes, and vaginal dryness, and it also has been thought to offer some protection from cardiovascular disease and osteoporosis, although the benefit of HRT for heart disease has recently been called into question.

Many women object to taking synthetic hormones because of unpleasant side effects, such as acne, breast soreness, headaches, and nausea. More dangerously, conventional hormone replacement therapy puts a woman at greater risk for blood clots, breast cancer, gallbladder disease, and high blood pressure. There are natural hormones available that have a far lower risk of side effects, and these hormones can be formulated in the precise combination that your body requires. If you are interested in natural hormone replacement therapy, consult a naturopathic doctor, or one who practices a holistic approach.

There's no doubt that the considerable hormonal shifts taking place in your body at this time are responsible for the symptoms of menopause. But you can greatly influence your passage through menopause in a positive way, and lessen your symptoms by eating well, getting regular exercise and plenty of rest, using nutritional supplements and herbs to help regulate your hormones, and taking time for yourself. First, it's helpful to understand what is taking place in your changing body.

Understanding Menopause

Menopause is the cessation of menstruation, and is

marked by the final menstrual period. But menopause actually encompasses the years prior to menopause when your hormones begin to shift in preparation for menopause (a stage referred to as perimenopause) and the year or two following the final menstrual cycle.

By the time most women reach their mid-forties, ovulation becomes erratic and the ovaries slow down their production of both estrogen and progesterone. One of the first signs of decreased hormone levels is erratic menstrual cycles. Most women find that their menstrual periods are initially more frequent and heavier, and then, as they move toward menopause, their cycles become lighter and further apart. Skipping a month or two, and then resuming menstruation is also common.

It's significant to note that your ovaries are responsible for producing not only estrogen and progesterone, but also for making other hormones called androgens, such as testosterone and DHEA. Although the ovaries do not produce estrogen or progesterone after menopause, they do continue producing androgens. Androgens are also made by other organs and glands, primarily the adrenal glands. These hormones are necessary for muscle tone, sex drive, and overall well-being. In addition, androgens

Androgens
Hormones produced by the adrenal glands that are essential for muscle tone, sex drive, and overall well-being.

are converted by fat cells into small amounts of estrogen, which helps to keep you healthy.

Your adrenal glands become extremely important in the menopausal years. When your ovaries slow down and eventually stop making hormones, your adrenal glands fill in the gap by taking over the production of hormones. Although the amount they produce is small in comparison to the amount once generated by the ovaries, they make enough to ease the transition through menopause and keep you vital for the rest of your life.

The Key to Vitality

Unfortunately, many women enter the menopausal years with less-than-optimal adrenal function. One of the roles of the adrenal glands is to help the body respond to physical and emotional stressors. But our bodies were not meant to be continually bombarded with the level of tension that is typical of modern life, and the adrenals become exhausted trying to maintain balance under conditions of recurring stress. As a result, the adrenal glands are overworked, and by the time most women reach menopause, their adrenals are not up to the task of generating sufficient hormones to maintain health and vitality.

Common symptoms of adrenal depletion include depression, fatigue, hypoglycemia, insomnia, lowered immunity, and poor concentration. With care, however, you can rebuild the health of your adrenal glands.

Any steps you can take to reduce stress in your life will help to ease the demands on your adrenals. Rest and sufficient sleep are also essential. And it is advisable to avoid caffeine and refined sugars, which provide a temporary boost of energy, but further deplete your adrenals.

One of the most significant dietary changes you can make is to cut down on sodium and eat at least seven servings of fresh vegetables and fruits daily. This will help restore a healthy balance of potassium and sodium, which supports adrenal health. In addition, eat frequent small meals with plenty of high-quality proteins, such as chicken, eggs, and fish, and take a high-potency multivitamin and mineral supplement daily. The B-complex vitamins, vitamin C, magnesium, and zinc are especially important for adrenal health. Take 50–100 mg of B-complex, 500 mg of vitamin C, 400 mg of magnesium, and 25 mg of zinc daily.

An Herbal Energy Tonic

Siberian ginseng (*Eleutherococcus senticosus*) is an excellent herb for helping to rebuild adrenal health. For centuries, it has been used in traditional Chinese medicine to enhance energy and vitality, and is prescribed as a longevity tonic. In the former Soviet Union, Siberian ginseng was studied extensively and the Soviet scientists noted its ability to help the body adapt to physical and emotional stressors. Siberian ginseng is approved by the German Commission E (a regulatory agency similar to the U.S. Food and Drug Administration) for the treatment of fatigue and debility.

To obtain its full benefits, the herb must be taken for two to three months, and it can be taken indefinitely. Although Siberian ginseng is very safe, taking higher-than-recommended doses can cause anxiety, insomnia, and irritability. If you don't feel a noticeable difference in energy within a couple of months, you may be taking an inferior product. Buy from reputable herb companies, or look for extracts standardized for eleutherosides, which are considered to be the active ingredient. Take one gram of powdered root, 1/2 teaspoon of fluid extract, or 100 mg of standardized extract two times daily.

Dietary Guidelines for Menopause

At midlife, the foods you choose to eat (and those you avoid) have a significant effect on how your body adapts to the changes of menopause. Your diet also influences your health and well-being in the years to come. It's essential at menopause to pay close attention to your diet, and to choose foods that are concentrated sources of health-supporting nutrients.

Certain foods have a profound effect on hormone levels, particularly foods that are rich in phytoestrogens. Phytoestrogens are plant compounds with weak estrogenic properties—they're approximately

fifty times weaker than estrogen. But these compounds are similar enough to
estrogen that they are able to
attach to receptor sites in the
body that are normally occu-
pied by estrogen.

> **Phytoestrogens**
> *Plant compounds
> with weak estrogen
> properties that can
> help balance estrogen
> levels in the body.*

If you have an excess of
estrogen (which causes such
menopausal symptoms as hot flashes), phytoestrogens help to reduce estrogen levels. If, on the other
hand, you are at risk for osteoporosis (low estrogen is
a contributing factor), phytoestrogens help to protect
you by providing some estrogenic activity.

Many foods are rich in phytoestrogens, and it
makes sense to include several servings of these helpful foods in your daily diet. Apples, celery, flaxseeds,
legumes, nuts, and whole grains are all good sources
of phytoestrogens. Of special value during menopause are soybeans and the products made from
them, such as soymilk, tempeh, and tofu. Researchers
believe the reason Japanese women have an easier
time during menopause, and
a significantly lower rate of
breast cancer than American
women, is their high consumption of soy products. Soy is a
rich source of phytoestrogens
called isoflavones, which are
available in supplement form.

> **Isoflavones**
> *A type of
> phytoestrogen (plant
> estrogen) that occurs
> abundantly in soy and
> can be of benefit
> to women.*

But it's best to include soy in your diet in the form of foods, such as soymilk, tempeh, or tofu, instead of using supplements of concentrated isoflavones. Although a daily serving (one cup of soymilk or one-half cup of tempeh or tofu) of soy foods is protective for your health, no one is certain of the effects of large doses of concentrated isoflavones. Some researchers have expressed concern that high doses of isoflavones may contribute to estrogen-dependent cancers, such as certain forms of breast cancer.

Essential fatty acids are also important during the menopausal years. Foods rich in omega-3 fatty acids help to keep hair, skin, and vaginal tissues healthy, and they aid in hormonal balance. Good sources of omega-3 fats are cold-water fish, such as salmon and sardines, and flaxseeds and walnuts. During menopause, it's a good idea to supplement your diet with one tablespoon of flaxseed oil daily to ensure sufficient amounts of omega-3 essential fatty acids. Vitamin E is also helpful for keeping vaginal tissues healthy; take 400–800 IU daily.

Herbal Help for Menopause

Women have traditionally relied on herbs to help ease the transition through menopause. As mentioned previously, Siberian ginseng helps to build vitality and strengthen the adrenal glands. Other herbs that are helpful for balancing hormones include chasteberry and black cohosh (*Cimicifuga racemosa*). Chasteberry increases progesterone levels by enhancing the activity of the pituitary gland, and is particularly effective for women who suffer from PMS-like symptoms associated with menopause.

Black cohosh has estrogenic-like activity, and helps ease such menopausal symptoms as depression, headaches, heart palpitations, hot flashes, irritability, night sweats, and vaginal atrophy. In at least twenty clinical studies, black cohosh has been shown to be as effective as synthetic estrogen for relieving menopausal symptoms. Symptom relief is not immediate, but black cohosh is far safer than synthetic hormones and has no toxicity or harmful side effects, other than occasional minor stomach upset. In a German multicenter study of 629 women, 80 percent of the women reported improvement of their symptoms within six to eight weeks.

Clinical studies have generally used extracts of black cohosh standardized for triterpenes, with the typical dosage equal to 4 mg of triterpenes daily. Black cohosh can also be taken as a liquid extract, approximately ½ teaspoon twice daily, or one 500–600 mg capsule of the powdered herb three times a day.

Supplements for Menopause

- High-potency multivitamin and mineral supplement, supplying:
  - B-complex: 50–100 mg daily

- Vitamin C: 500 mg daily

- Vitamin E: 400–800 IU daily

- Calcium: 1,200 mg daily

- Magnesium: 400 mg daily

- Zinc: 25 mg daily

- Flaxseed oil: 1 tablespoon daily

- Black cohosh: approximately $\frac{1}{2}$ teaspoon liquid extract, or one 500–600 mg capsule of the powdered herb, two to three times daily

- Chasteberry: $\frac{1}{2}$ teaspoon liquid extract or one 500–600 mg capsule three times daily

- Siberian ginseng: one gram powdered root, $\frac{1}{2}$ teaspoon fluid extract, or 100 mg standardized extract two times daily

CHAPTER 4

PREVENTING
OSTEOPOROSIS

One out of every four postmenopausal women will be faced with a diagnosis of osteoporosis, and more than 45,000 women will die this year from injuries related to weakened bones, such as fractures of the hip and spine. Equally tragic is the crippling loss of mobility that occurs with osteoporosis. There are a number of specific risk factors that predispose a woman to osteoporosis, including heredity. But while you can't control your genetic heritage, you can control the other risk factors that contribute to bone loss.

Osteoporosis: Risk Factors for Women

- Excessive alcohol or caffeine intake

- High phosphorus intake

- High protein or sodium diet

- Lack of vitamin D

- Low calcium intake

- Menopause

- Sedentary lifestyle

- Smoking

- Thin build, particularly for those of Northern European or Asian descent

The Basics of Bone Health

Bones are dense, hard structures, but they are continually in the process of being broken down and recreated. Your bones are a storehouse for calcium in your body, a mineral that is vital for a variety of essential body processes. Calcium reserves are drawn upon to keep bones and teeth strong, to regulate heartbeat and muscle contractions, to transmit nerve impulses, and to aid in blood clotting.

Childhood and early adulthood are critical times for building healthy bone. Ideally, young women will have optimal nutrition and plenty of exercise to help them build a strong bone structure that will carry them into their later years. Unfortunately, many young women diet excessively, don't get enough exercise, and don't obtain sufficient amounts of nutrients for maximum bone strength. By the time a woman reaches thirty, her bones have achieved their greatest density; after the age of about thirty-five, more bone is being withdrawn than replaced.

At menopause, bone loss escalates when levels of estrogen decline, because estrogen plays an important role in regulating the ability of the bones to absorb calcium. But it's not all hormonally driven. A poor diet and a sedentary lifestyle greatly intensify the process of bone loss, and it's these factors that make or break bone strength. If your diet is rich in calcium and other necessary bone-building nutrients, and if you exercise regularly, your body will deposit calcium into your bones and your bones will grow stronger.

Factors in Bone Loss

Factors that accelerate bone loss include dieting, nutrient deficiencies, smoking, and excess alcohol, caffeine, phosphorus, protein, and sodium. Dieting, or trying to be too thin, is harmful to bone health at any age. Low-calorie diets are often deficient in calcium and other essential nutrients, and the body tries to make up for the lack by taking calcium from the bones to perform necessary metabolic functions. In addition, if you are very thin, you are at higher risk for osteoporosis because fat reserves in the hips and thighs are essential for the production of estrogen after menopause.

In general, the habits that are harmful to your general health are also harmful to your bones. Smokers are at greater risk for osteoporosis than non-smokers: they tend to go through menopause (which decreases levels of estrogen) earlier and smoking suppresses the activity of the parathyroid glands, which are responsible for regulating calcium levels. Excessive amounts of alcohol, caffeine, or sodium increase the amount of calcium that is lost in the urine, and this weakens the bones.

Too much protein can also leach calcium from the bones. Although your body needs the amino acids in proteins to make bone from calcium, too much protein creates an acidic condition in the blood that must be neutralized—and calcium is used in this process. It's best to limit your protein intake to no more than about eight ounces per day, and to choose vegetable proteins, such as tempeh and tofu, as well as animal proteins. While you don't have to become a vegetarian to avoid osteoporosis, it's worthwhile to note that research has shown that women who eat a balanced vegetarian diet have the least incidence of osteoporosis, while women who eat a diet high in meat sustain the highest rate of bone loss.

An often overlooked factor in osteoporosis is the mineral phosphorus. Phosphorus is necessary for building bone, and we need about twice as much calcium as phosphorus for optimal calcium absorption. But if more phosphorus than calcium is consumed, a bone-dissolving hormone is secreted to maintain the proper calcium-to-phosphorus ratio in the bloodstream. Unfortunately, our diets are not only lacking in sufficient calcium, but they are loaded with phosphorus—dairy products, meats, nuts, poultry, seafood, seeds, and whole grains contain significant amounts of phosphorus. Many processed foods, such as baked goods, also contain phosphorus, and carbonated soft drinks contain large amounts of phosphoric acid. When the numbers are tallied, most women take in four times as much phosphorus as calcium.

To decrease the risk of osteoporosis, conventional doctors tend to rely on drug therapy, often prescribing hormone replacement therapy (HRT). But HRT is not appropriate for women who have a history of breast or uterine cancer, cardiovascular disease, diabetes, gallbladder disease, liver disease, or migraine headaches. Bone-building drugs such as Fosamax (alendronate sodium) are also commonly prescribed to slow the rate of bone loss. However, these drugs can cause serious digestive problems, including constipation, diarrhea, nausea, severe heartburn, stomach pain, and even ulceration of the esophagus. It takes more effort to build bone with diet and lifestyle changes, but the only side effects are positive ones that enhance your overall well-being.

Dietary Recommendations for Strong Bones

When you think of eating for strong bones, the first thing that probably comes to mind is milk. But although milk is a good source of calcium, and calcium is an essential nutrient for bone health, simply drinking milk is not going to protect your bones. In fact, researchers who evaluated the dietary intake of 78,000 women over a twelve-year period (part of the long-term Harvard Nurses' Health Study) found that those women who had a higher intake of calcium from dairy foods did not have a decreased risk of bone fractures. Despite what the dairy industry would have you believe, the truth is that strong bones are not only related to how much calcium you are getting from your diet, but are also dependent upon how well you are absorbing calcium. To prevent osteoporosis, you need to supply your body with all the essential nutrients for strong bones, avoid foods that contribute to bone loss, and optimize your digestion to aid in the absorption of nutrients, including calcium.

In addition to calcium, the nutrients that are essential for building bone include magnesium, vitamins D and K, zinc, and the trace minerals boron, copper, and manganese. Eating a varied diet, including at least seven servings a day of fresh fruits and vegetables, is the best way to obtain most of these nutrients. For additional insurance, you should also take a high-potency multivitamin and mineral supplement that includes trace minerals.

Dairy products are good sources of calcium, but there are some problems associated with them. Dairy foods are high in phosphorus and protein, both of which can contribute to bone loss if there are excessive amounts in the diet. In addition, many women are lactose intolerant, and experience abdominal cramps, bloating, and diarrhea when they eat dairy foods. Fermented dairy products, such as yogurt, are generally better tolerated because they contain beneficial bacteria that aid in digestion. But there's no reason to rely primarily on dairy to meet your calcium requirements. There are many other calcium-rich foods to choose from, including almonds, broccoli, canned salmon or sardines with bones, dark leafy green vegetables (such as collards, kale, and mustard greens), and tofu processed with calcium.

Dark leafy green vegetables are not only rich in calcium, but they are also an excellent source of vitamin K, a nutrient that is critical for bone formation and for regulating levels of calcium in the blood. About half the vitamin K you need is produced by helpful bacteria in the intestinal tract. You can optimize your body's production of vitamin K by maintaining a healthy population of friendly bacteria in your intestinal tract, and eating yogurt that contains live acidophilus cultures is a good way to do this. You can also obtain beneficial intestinal flora through supplements. Take supplements that supply at least 5–10 billion viable *Lactobacillus acidophilus* and *Bifidobacterium bifidum* daily for at least one month.

Soy foods are especially helpful for protecting against bone loss. Tofu can be an excellent source of calcium if it is processed with calcium, but more importantly, soy foods are rich in isoflavones, natural compounds that have estrogenic effects and help to build bone. But while studies have shown that soy isoflavones help to increase bone density and slow the rate of bone loss, concentrated supplements of isoflavones may not be helpful, and can be harmful. A 2001 study published in the *Journal of the American Medical Association* showed that ipriflavone, a commonly prescribed isoflavone supplement, did not prevent bone loss and, in addition, lowered white blood cell counts.

Instead of turning to concentrated supplements, it seems prudent to rely on whole foods, such as soymilk, tempeh, and tofu to get your protective ration of isoflavones. For bone health, eat one or two servings of soy daily (one cup of soymilk, or four ounces of tempeh or tofu equals one serving).

Supplements for Strong Bones

To insure that you're getting enough calcium, it's a good idea to take a calcium supplement in addition to eating calcium-rich foods. There are many different forms of calcium available, but calcium citrate is probably the most easily absorbable form. It's important to avoid supplements made from bone meal, dolomite, and oyster shell. They are poorly absorbed, and are likely to be contaminated with lead, which is highly toxic and accumulates in the body. If you eat at least two or three servings of calcium-rich foods daily, a supplemental dosage of 1,000 mg of calcium is sufficient. If you don't get enough calcium in your diet, then aim for 1,500 mg daily. For best absorption, take calcium supplements with meals, and don't take more than 500 mg at a time.

Magnesium is another nutrient necessary for bone strength. It's found in a variety of foods, such as leafy greens, legumes, nuts, seeds, and whole grains. But there are many factors that deplete magnesium, including alcohol, and emotional and physical stress. And many women don't eat sufficient amounts of magnesium-rich foods. To provide adequate levels of magnesium, take 600 mg of magnesium daily in an easily absorbable form, such as aspartate, citrate, gluconate, or lactate.

Getting enough calcium in your diet is only part of the strategy for maintaining healthy bones. You also need to ensure that you're absorbing the calcium you ingest. Vitamin D aids the absorption of calcium in the gastrointestinal tract, and it also helps to maintain adequate levels of calcium in the blood for building bone. Your body makes vitamin D, but it needs sunlight to do so. When your skin is exposed to sunlight, a cholesterol compound in your skin is transformed into vitamin D. But many women get little or no sun exposure, and clothing, glass, smog, and sunscreens all block the rays that produce vitamin D. Only a few foods contain vitamin D—primarily butter, eggs, and fortified milk—all things that many women may not regularly eat.

The best way to get this essential vitamin is through moderate sun exposure; about fifteen minutes in direct early morning or late afternoon sunlight three days a week is sufficient. It's also a good idea to take a supplement of 400 IU of vitamin D daily, which is the amount that is found in most multivitamins. While you want to be certain that you're getting enough, vitamin D is not something that you want to get too much of because an excess of this vitamin can contribute to heart disease, kidney damage, and tissue calcification.

The Importance of Exercise

No matter how healthful your diet is, exercise is a necessity for building and maintaining strong bones. A sedentary lifestyle is clearly linked to osteoporosis, and studies have shown that as little as one week of bed rest weakens bones. But the good news is that bones become stronger when they are stressed by moderate weight-bearing activity. When you engage in weight-bearing exercise, a mild electrical charge is generated in your body that causes more calcium to be deposited in the bones. If your dietary intake of calcium is adequate, then your body has calcium available to fortify your bones.

It's important to realize that not all exercise is helpful for strengthening bones. For exercise to be beneficial, it has to stress your bones to trigger the necessary electrical charge. Weight-bearing exercises, such as walking, dancing, and strenuous yoga are excellent. Make sure to also include activities that involve your upper body, such as gardening, rowing, and cross-country skiing. If you find it challenging to regularly engage in physical activities that involve both lower and upper body exercises, try a simple exercise program that uses hand-held weights, or join a gym that has weight-training equipment.

To keep your bones strong, you should engage in at least thirty minutes of weight-bearing exercise five times per week. Even if you have been diagnosed with osteoporosis, you should be exercising regularly. Weight-bearing exercise can slow down the rate of bone loss, and it can help to build stronger bones.

Exercising throughout your life is essential for remaining strong and vital into old age. People often become frail and weak, not because of aging, but because they have stopped using their bodies. When muscles weaken, coordination usually deteriorates as well. The stronger you are and the more confident you are in your body, the less likely you are to have an accident such as a fall.

Supplements for Preventing Osteoporosis

- High-potency multivitamin and mineral supplement daily that includes:

  - Calcium: 1,000–1,500 mg daily

  - Magnesium: 600 mg daily

  - Vitamin D: 400 IU daily

- Probiotic formula: 5–10 billion viable *Lactobacillus acidophilus* and *Bifidobacterium bifidum* daily (to promote vitamin K)

CHAPTER 5

PREVENTING CANCER

According to the American Cancer Society, approximately one-third of all women will be stricken with cancer at some time in life. Because there are at least 200 different types of cancer, it's unlikely that there will ever be one single drug or vaccine that will offer protection from this dreaded disease. But even though cancer appears in so many forms and can be so challenging to treat, cancer cells have a lot in common with one another—they all begin when something in normal cell replication goes awry. And many of the reasons that cells replicate abnormally and become cancerous are within our control.

Researchers estimate that one-third of all cancer deaths in the U.S. are related to dietary factors, and another third are caused by cigarette smoking. Clearly, these are factors over which you have influence. Our bodies have marvelous built-in mechanisms for searching out and destroying cells that have gone astray. By supporting your body's natural processes of healing, and by avoiding the toxins that contribute to the formation of mutant cells, you can do a great deal to protect yourself from cancer.

How Cancer Arises

It's important to understand that your body is perfectly equipped to handle cancerous cells. Your cells are constantly replicating—approximately 10 million cells are replaced every second in your body. With so much activity, it's not uncommon for a cell to occasionally turn out a faulty reproduction.

Free Radical
An unstable molecule that occurs normally in the body, or as a byproduct of environmental factors, and causes cellular damage.

In addition, cells are continually bombarded by substances that can damage DNA, which is the cellular blueprint for cell reproduction. Cellular injury is often caused by free radicals, which are unstable molecules created as a result of normal metabolic processes, and by environmental factors, such as exposure to cigarette smoke, excessive sunlight, pesticides, and pollution.

When abnormal cells arise, they must be destroyed to keep them from creating additional flawed cells. The job of finding and destroying deviant cells falls to the immune system, where specialized white blood cells hunt for abnormal cells, and eradicate them before they have the opportunity to reproduce. In addition, any cell that begins to multiply uncontrollably is programmed to self-destruct.

Most of the time, these built-in methods of protection are sufficient to prevent the development of cancer. But sometimes, the immune system loses its ability to recognize and destroy cancerous cells, and defective cells can multiply out-of-control. The immune system can also be overwhelmed by large amounts of abnormal cells and not be able to provide adequate protection. Enhancing the ability of your immune system to defend you against the development of cancer is critical.

How to Strengthen Your Immune System

Your immune system is an intricate network of glands, organs, and specialized cells that work together to protect your well-being. The essential components of the immune system include an extensive arrangement of lymph nodes scattered throughout the body, bone marrow, the spleen, the thymus gland, and a variety of white blood cells and other blood elements. It's a complex and magnificient structure, and one that scientists are still learning about. One thing is certain: Your immune system is your first line of defense against cancer, and strengthening your immunity requires a holistic approach that includes diet, exercise, supplements, and a healthy lifestyle. Let's take a closer look at these factors.

One of the primary causes of depressed immunity is a diet lacking in sufficient nutrients. Adequate amounts of protein are necessary for proper immune function, but too much protein can impair immunity. The optimal amount for a healthy immune system is approximately eight ounces of chicken, eggs, fish, tofu, turkey, or other high-quality proteins daily. Avoid commercially produced meats and dairy foods because they often contain residues of antibiotics, which are harmful to the immune system. In addition to protein, eat a wide variety of fresh fruits and vegetables, legumes, nuts, seeds, and whole grains to provide your immune system with an array of vitamins, minerals, and trace nutrients. As much as possible, eat organic foods to avoid the toxic chemicals that are found in commercially produced foods.

What you avoid eating also plays a critical role in the health of your immune system. A diet high in hydrogenated oils, polyunsaturated oils, and saturated fats impairs the functioning of your immune system. And sugar and other concentrated sweeteners can significantly hinder your immune system's capabilities. Studies have shown that even one serving of a sugary food can inhibit immune function for several hours.

Exercise helps to strengthen your immune system in several ways. Approximately thirty to forty-five minutes of moderate exercise, such as brisk walking, has been proven to increase immune activity, relieve stress, and improve lymphatic circulation, all of which enhance immunity. Studies have shown that women who exercise at least four hours a week have a significantly lower risk of breast cancer than women who do not exercise. This may be because exercise helps to regulate estrogen levels. Exercise also boosts mood, which has a positive effect on immune function.

But despite all of the benefits attributed to exercise, it is possible to overdo it. Extremely stressful exercise, such as training for a marathon, has been shown to deplete the immune response. If you are involved in a very strenuous exercise program, you should be careful to get enough rest, allow your body sufficient time to recover after training, and take supplements and herbs that support your immune system.

Getting enough sleep is also essential for keeping your immune system strong. In order to function properly, your body and your immune system need a minimum of seven hours of sleep every night. During sleep, powerful immune-enhancing compounds are released. If you are sleep-deprived, all aspects of your immunity are impaired, and you are more likely to succumb to a virus or other infection. Chronic sleep-deprivation can significantly affect your immune system's ability to protect you from cancer. In our fast-paced world, it's often challenging to make time for sufficient rest and relaxation. But failing to provide your body with time for restoration and rejuvenation creates a state of chronic physical and emotional stress that is one of the primary causes of immune weakness.

A number of research studies have proven that emotional stress has a measurable effect on immunity. During times of stress, adrenal hormones that suppress immune function are released. Living in a continual state of stress wears down your immune system and leaves you much more susceptible to everything from the common cold to cancer. While a stress-filled life that negatively affects your physical and emotional well-being is often accepted as normal, it's certainly not a healthy way to live.

Learning to manage stress is one of the most powerful steps you can take to support your immune system and your overall health. It's important to find ways of relieving stress that are effective for you. Exercise can be a great stress-reliever, as can breathing exercises, meditation, prayer, and yoga. Cultivating close relationships with friends and family also plays a role in building a strong immune system because having people with whom you can share your deepest feelings and concerns is a tremendous stress-reliever and enhances overall well-being.

The Importance of Avoiding Toxins

No matter how committed you are to a healthful diet and lifestyle, we are all exposed to a large number of potentially carcinogenic toxins on a daily basis.

Some of these toxins are environmental pollutants,

some are diet-related, and some arise internally as byproducts of natural metabolic processes. These toxins trigger the formation of free radicals, which damage healthy cells and can result in cancerous changes. It's impossible to completely avoid contact with toxic substances, because you don't have control over environmental pollutants, nor can you stop the metabolic processes of your body that generate toxins. But you can limit your exposure to toxic substances as much as possible, and you can decrease your body's production of toxins through diet and supplements.

Researchers are finding that many chemicals in the environment, such as hormones in dairy products and meats, pesticides, and pollutants, have estrogenlike activity. These chemicals are referred to as hormonal disrupters, or xenoestrogens, and are suspected of playing a role in hormonally triggered cancers, such as breast cancer and uterine cancer.

> **Xenoestrogen**
> *A chemical toxin that acts like estrogen and disrupts hormonal activity in the body.*

Some plastics can also be hormonal disrupters, especially the plastic wrap used by most supermarkets for wrapping cheese, fish, poultry, and meat. It contains a chemical known as DEHA, which readily migrates into food. To be safe, avoid buying foods wrapped in plastic, and never microwave foods in plastic wrap or plastic containers.

Other actions you can take to decrease your exposure to toxins include avoiding unnecessary exposure to radiation, choosing natural alternatives to chemical household and garden products, drinking filtered water, and eating organic foods. Of course, it's absolutely essential to avoid tobacco smoke, which accounts for one-third of all cancer deaths. It's also a good idea to limit your alcohol intake to no more than one drink per day. If you are at high risk for breast cancer, it's probably best to refrain completely from drinking alcohol. Some research indicates that even small amounts of alcohol are associated with an increased incidence of breast cancer.

Prevent Cancer with Fruits and Vegetables

As previously discussed, eating a diet rich in protective nutrients is vitally important for healthy immune functioning. Because diet is targeted as being responsible for one-third of all cancers, it makes sense to understand, as much as possible, how to safeguard your health through nutrition. One of the most important dietary changes you can make is to increase the amount of fresh fruits and vegetables that you eat. Fresh fruits and vegetables are the richest sources of antioxidants, which help to neutralize free radical damage. In addition, these foods contain other

> **Phytochemicals**
> *Compounds in plants, such as flavonoids and carotenoids, that have protective, disease-preventing properties.*

protective phytochemicals, including flavonoids and carotenoids.

Try to eat at least seven servings of fresh fruits and vegetables every day, and preferably strive for ten servings. A serving is one-half cup of a vegetable, one cup of leafy greens, one average-size piece of fruit, one-half cup of fruit, or six ounces of fresh fruit or vegetable juice. To get a wide range of protective nutrients, vary the fruits and vegetables you eat and choose those that have the deepest, richest colors—for example, choose dark green leafy romaine or red lettuce over pale iceberg lettuce and dark purple grapes over green grapes. A variety of color in your choices will provide a variety of beneficial nutrients.

Certain vegetables and fruits contain special protective compounds, and it's worthwhile to include these foods in your diet as often as possible. Broccoli, cabbage, cauliflower, collards, kale, and other members of the cruciferous family are rich in beneficial sulfur compounds called indoles; cruciferous vegetables

> **Glutathione**
> *A powerful detoxifying and antioxidant compound made by the body and found in some foods, including those in the cruciferous vegetable family.*

also enhance the production of glutathione, which helps to neutralize carcinogens. Garlic, onions, scallions, and other members of the allium family improve immune activity and increase the levels of the enzymes that break down carcinogens.

Foods rich in vitamin C and beta-carotene have potent antioxidant activity. Broccoli, citrus fruits, red peppers, and strawberries are all good sources of vitamin C. Dark leafy green vegetables and deep yellow-orange fruits and vegetables, such as apricots, cantaloupe, carrots, and sweet potatoes, are high in beta-carotene, which may help to reverse precancerous changes in cells.

Eating a variety of fruits and vegetables ensures that you are providing your cells with a comprehensive array of cancer-fighting phytonutrients, such as ellagic acid, limonene, and lycopene. Apples, grapes, raspberries, and strawberries contain ellagic acid; lemons, limes, and oranges are rich in limonene; and carrots, red peppers, tomatoes, and watermelon are good sources of lycopene.

Other Dietary Suggestions for Cancer Prevention

Because experts estimate that at least one-third of all cancers are directly related to diet, it makes sense to eat as healthfully as possible. In addition to eating generous amounts of fruits and vegetables, the most important dietary steps you can take to prevent cancer are to choose healthful fats, including omega-3 fatty acids, consume plenty of fiber, drink green tea, and eat soy foods daily.

Current research indicates that the *type* of fat you eat is much more important than the *amount* of fat in your diet. Hydrogenated oils, polyunsaturated oils, and saturated fats have all been associated with an increased risk of cancer. These types of fats have been found to generate large numbers of cell-damaging free radicals; they also create chemicals in the intestinal tract that are converted by bacteria into harmful types of estrogen involved in breast and reproductive cancers.

Worst of all are hydrogenated or partially hydrogenated oils; they contain trans-fatty acids, a particularly harmful fat to your cells. Trans-fatty acids are created during a chemical process known as hydrogenation during which oils are made solid or semi-solid at room temperature. Hydrogenated and partially hydrogenated fats are found in many margarines, vegetable shortenings, and baked goods and processed foods made with these fats. Polyunsaturated oils, such as corn, safflower, soybean, and sunflower oils, are highly susceptible to oxidation (which creates cell-damaging free radicals) when exposed to air, heat, and light. It is impossible to keep these oils from turning rancid in your kitchen, and most of the time, they have already started to oxidize before they leave the store shelves. Saturated fats are found in large amounts in full-fat dairy products, poultry skin, red meat, and tropical oils, such as coconut and palm oils. It's best to minimize these foods in your diet.

Now for the good news about fats. Certain types of fats, especially olive oil and omega-3 fats, are beneficial for your health and help protect against cancer. Olive oil is a monounsaturated fat that makes your cell membranes more resistant to the destructive effects of free radicals. In large population studies of Mediterranean cultures, a high intake of olive oil has been associated with their remarkably low rates of cancer. The premium type is extra-virgin olive oil. It's made from the first pressing of olives, has the best flavor, and contains the most protective nutrients.

Omega-3 fats, found in cold-water fish, flaxseed, and walnuts, also help to protect cell membranes and inhibit the development of cancerous cells. In a recent study in Tours, France, reported in the *International Journal of Cancer,* 241 women with breast cancer and 88 women with benign breast disease had samples of breast tissue taken during surgery; the fatty tissue was then examined for omega-3 fatty acid content (the body stores omega-3 fats and other fats in fatty tissues, such as breast tissue). The researchers found that those women with higher levels of omega-3 fats in their tissues had a significantly lower incidence of breast cancer. Omega-3 fats have also been shown to be protective against other types of cancers.

> **Lignans**
> A type of phyto-estrogen, found in flaxseeds, that helps protect against breast cancer and other cancers.

To saturate your cells with these beneficial fatty acids, eat two to three servings of cold-water fish, such as salmon and sardines, weekly; a small handful of walnuts several times a week; and take one tablespoon of flaxseed oil, or one tablespoon of freshly ground flaxseeds daily. Ground flaxseeds and specially processed flaxseed oil are rich sources of lignans, compounds that help to inhibit the growth of estrogen-related cancers.

Never heat or cook with flaxseed oil, but instead, add it to salad dressings, or pour it onto baked potatoes, pasta, vegetables, or other dishes.

Soy foods are extremely beneficial in helping to prevent cancer. Soybeans contain compounds called protease inhibitors, which block the action of enzymes that stimulate tumor growth.

> **Protease Inhibitor**
> *Plant compounds found in soybeans that block the action of enzymes that stimulate tumor growth.*

The anticancer substances found in soy foods work to block cancer in several ways. They inhibit the development of blood vessels that feed tumors and make them grow, they speed up the death of cancer cells, and they help break down carcinogens in the body. Soy foods are especially helpful for women. They contain a natural plant estrogen called genistein, which blocks estrogen from causing cancerous changes in hormone-sensitive tissues, such as the breasts. To reap the cancer-protective benefits of soybeans, consume four ounces of soy foods, such as tempeh or tofu, or one cup of soy milk daily.

Few women obtain sufficient dietary fiber, and yet

fiber is essential for preventing cancer. A fiber-rich diet helps move waste products efficiently through the intestinal tract, and keeps toxins from lingering in the body. Fiber has the additional benefit of helping to reduce levels of harmful estrogen because it binds to this estrogen in the intestinal tract and prevents it from being reabsorbed into the bloodstream. For optimal protection, eat between twenty-five and thirty-five grams of fiber daily. Some of the best sources of fiber include fruits, legumes, and vegetables. If your diet falls short of providing sufficient fiber, you can increase your intake with fiber supplements made from flaxseeds, guar gum, pectin, and psyllium seed husks. Take between one and three tablespoons daily.

Green tea helps protect against cancer in more than one way. It contains compounds called polyphenols, which are potent antioxidants that prevent free radicals from damaging healthy cells.

Polyphenols
Potent antioxidants, found abundantly in green tea, that prevent free radicals from damaging healthy cells.

These compounds all support the body's efforts to eliminate carcinogens, improve the cells' resistance to cancer-causing substances, and help prevent cancer cells from multiplying. Researchers believe that one compelling reason the Japanese have a significantly lower incidence of cancer is their daily habit of drinking green tea. To obtain the protective benefits of green tea, drink at least three cups daily. Since green tea has a subtle flavor that can quickly turn bitter if it is steeped for too long, to get the best flavor, you should bring water to a boil, let it cool slightly before pouring it over the tea, then steep it no longer than three minutes. If you prefer, you can use a standardized extract of green tea. Take approximately 400 mg daily of an extract standardized to 90 percent polyphenols.

Supplements for Preventing Cancer

Dietary supplements provide a concentrated source of nutrients that help strengthen your immune system and protect your cells from cancer-causing substances. For starters, it's a good idea to take a high-potency multivitamin and mineral supplement to provide your immune system with the nutrients it needs to function optimally. The supplement should contain 50 mg of B-vitamin complex, including 400 mcg of folic acid, which helps prevent cervical dysplasia, a potential precursor to uterine cancer. It should also contain 400 IU of vitamin D because a clear relationship has been established between a deficiency of vitamin D and breast cancer.

Make sure that your multivitamin supplement supplies a variety of antioxidants, including beta-carotene and mixed carotenoids (25,000 IU), vitamin C (500 mg), vitamin E (400–800 IU), selenium (200 mcg), and zinc (25 mg). If your multivitamin and mineral falls short of these recommendations, take additional supplements to fill the gap. In addition, CoQ_{10} has potent antioxidant properties. Take 30–60 mg daily.

Herbal Help for Immune Support

Herbs can be valuable allies in protecting your immune system and helping ward off cancer. Some of the most potent protective herbs are found in Chinese medicine, which has a long tradition of using herbs to strengthen immunity.

Astragalus (*Astragalus membranaceous*) is a fibrous root that has proven effective for increasing immune activity, and is also prescribed for restoring immune function in people who have undergone radiation or chemotherapy. Maitake (*Grifola frondosa*), reishi (*Ganoderma lucidum*), and shiitake (*Lentinula edodes*) are all mushrooms with powerful immune-enhancing properties; they also inhibit the growth of cancer. All these herbs are available as extracts, or in capsules, and can be taken long-term for immune enhancement. Follow the manufacturer's dosage recommendations.

Supplements for Cancer Prevention

- High-potency multivitamin and mineral supplement daily that includes:

  - Beta-carotene with mixed carotenoids: 25,000 IU daily

  - Folic acid: 400 mcg daily

- Selenium: 200 mcg daily
- Vitamin C: 500–1,000 mg daily
- Vitamin D: 400 IU daily
- Vitamin E: 400–800 IU daily
- Zinc: 25 mg daily

- CoQ_{10}: 30–60 mg daily

- Flaxseed oil with lignans: 1 tablespoon daily

- Astragalus, maitake, reishi, or shiitake, for immune support: follow label instructions for dosages

- Green tea: three cups daily, or 400 mg of a standardized extract

CHAPTER 6

PREVENTING HEART DISEASE

Many people still have the misconception that heart disease is something that happens primarily to men. It's true that women are fortunate in having the natural heart-protective effects of estrogen prior to menopause. Estrogen helps to keep coronary arteries flexible, and also plays an important role in keeping cholesterol levels low. But during and after menopause, when estrogen levels naturally decline, the risk of heart disease for women increases dramatically. After menopause, women are more likely than men to be stricken with heart disease. In fact, cardiovascular disease is the leading cause of death for women, affecting one out of every three women over the age of sixty-five.

Recent studies have shown that hormone replacement therapy, which was long thought to provide cardiovascular protection for post-menopausal women, does not help to prevent heart disease, and is probably a bad idea for women who have a prior history of heart disease. A four-year study of 2,763 post-menopausal women with a history of heart disease, reported in the *Journal of the American Medical Association* in 1998, revealed that hormone replacement therapy *increased* cardiac risk during the first year of use. As a result, the American Heart Association recently recommended against hormone replacement therapy for the prevention of heart disease by women with a history of cardiovascular disease. As for healthy postmenopausal women, the association says there is insufficient evidence to indicate that hormone replacement therapy prevents heart disease.

Fortunately, with the proper diet, exercise, and supplements, there is a great deal you can do to keep your cardiovascular system healthy.

Heart Disease: Risk Factors for Women

- A family history of heart disease
- A high total cholesterol, high triglycerides, and a low HDL cholesterol
- A sedentary lifestyle
- Being over age sixty-five
- Being more than 20 percent over ideal weight
- Cigarette smoking
- Diabetes
- Entering menopause before age forty-five

- Having excess weight in the abdomen
- High blood pressure
- High levels of homocysteine
- High levels of stress

The Causes of Heart Disease

Heart attacks and strokes are the most common cardiovascular diseases. The primary contributing factors are atherosclerosis (a thickening and hardening of the arteries) and high blood pressure. Atherosclerosis occurs when the lining of an artery is injured by free radicals, unstable molecules that occur naturally in the body or can be initiated by exposure to environmental toxins, stress, or a virus. The body attempts to repair the damage, and in the process, cholesterol, other fats, and cellular debris all accumulate in

> **Atherosclerosis**
> *A thickening and hardening of the arteries, which can lead to heart attacks and strokes.*

the arteries and roughen the artery walls with plaque, at which point platelets and other compounds in the blood can stick to their surface and form a clot. The disease often progresses silently until arterial blockage causes a heart attack or stroke.

Although it would seem that lowering cholesterol levels is the most critical step for preventing atherosclerosis, it's not the only factor in the development of heart disease. High cholesterol levels can play a role in atherosclerosis, but not all people with high cholesterol have clogged arteries, and people with atherosclerosis can have cholesterol levels in the normal range.

However, conventional medical practitioners tend to focus on cholesterol, and usually prescribe cholesterol-lowering drugs. While these drugs do help to decrease cholesterol levels, they can have unpleasant and even dangerous side effects, including possible liver damage. A better approach is to focus on lowering your cholesterol naturally and protecting your arteries from free radical damage, at the same time identifying and reducing other risk factors.

Understanding Cholesterol

Cholesterol is a waxy, fatlike substance that is found in every cell of your body. Even if you were to eat a no-cholesterol diet, your body would still manufacture it, because cholesterol is essential for the production of bile, cell membranes, hormones, and vitamin D. Cholesterol only becomes a problem when too much of it accumulates in your bloodstream or arteries. Factors that contribute to this unhealthy buildup include a lack of dietary nutrients essential to the normal metabolism of cholesterol, poor liver function, or a sedentary lifestyle.

It's important to note that not all cholesterol is implicated in cardiovascular disease. A type of cholesterol called HDL (high-density lipoproteins) actually helps protect your arteries, and you want as much of this beneficial cholesterol as possible in your bloodstream. But for cardiovascular health, you want low levels of LDL cholesterol (low-density lipoproteins) and low levels of triglycerides (another type of blood fat).

Here's how cholesterol operates in your body: It is carried in your blood on molecules called lipoproteins. Low-density lipoproteins (LDL) transport cholesterol and triglycerides from your liver to your cells. While it's circulating through your bloodstream, cholesterol can accumulate on artery walls. High-density lipoproteins (HDL) pick up this cholesterol from the arteries and return it to the liver, where it is metabolized and eliminated.

> **Lipoproteins**
> *Molecules in the bloodstream that transport cholesterol and trigylcerides to and from your liver and your cells.*

Although high levels of LDL cholesterol and triglycerides are clearly associated with an increased risk of cardiovascular disease, people who have high levels of HDL cholesterol tend to have a low risk of clogged arteries. On the other hand, if your HDL levels are too low, you are at risk for cardiovascular disease, even if you have a low level of total cholesterol. For cardiovascular health, you should focus on lowering your LDL cholesterol and triglycerides while raising your HDL cholesterol. It's not as complicated as it sounds. Many of the lifestyle and dietary suggestions that lower harmful cholesterol also boost helpful cholesterol.

For optimal cardiovascular protection, your total cholesterol should be less than 200 mg/dl, your LDL no higher than 130 (preferably closer to 100), your triglycerides less than 150 mg/dl, and your HDL greater than 35. More important than the individual numbers in your cholesterol profile, however, is the ratio of your HDL cholesterol to your total cholesterol, and also the ratio of your LDL to HDL. This tells you how effectively your liver is metabolizing and eliminating cholesterol. The ideal ratio of total cholesterol to HDL is below 3.5, and the ratio of LDL to HDL should be no higher than 2.5.

Managing Blood Pressure

High blood pressure (also called hypertension) is the most common type of cardiovascular disease. A blood pressure reading of more than 140/90 puts you in the category of having hypertension, and greatly increases your risk of heart disease and stroke. The vast majority of the time, there is no physiological cause of high blood pressure. However, there are a number of factors that contribute to elevated blood pressure, principally a diet high in sodium or low in calcium, magnesium, and potassium, excessive alcohol intake, overweight—and stress.

Although doctors often prescribe drugs for controlling blood pressure, drugs can cause such side effects as dizziness and fatigue, and can increase levels of harmful cholesterol and triglycerides. It's far better to avoid drugs and adopt lifestyle changes, such as eating a healthful diet, exercising regularly, managing stress, and taking nutritional supplements and herbs. If you have hypertension, it's essential that you monitor your blood pressure regularly to make sure it is within a healthy range.

Other Risk Factors in Heart Disease

Although high cholesterol is generally regarded as the primary cause of cardiovascular disease, there are two other factors—homocysteine and fibrinogen—that should also be considered. Homocysteine, a byproduct of the metabolism of the amino acid methionine, is usually neutralized by your body into harmless compounds. But if you are deficient in folic acid, vitamin B_6, or vitamin B_{12}, homocysteine levels can increase to dangerous levels in the blood. Homocysteine damages arteries, increases the risk of blood clots, and promotes the buildup of cholesterol in arteries.

> **Homocysteine**
> *A byproduct of amino-acid metabolism that can be a risk factor in heart disease if there are high levels of it in the blood.*

You can generally obtain an adequate supply of B-vitamins by taking a B-complex supplement that supplies 400 mcg of folic acid, 50 mg of B_6, and 400 mcg of B_{12}. Some people, however, are genetically predisposed to high levels of homocysteine, and may have much greater requirements for B-vitamins than the recommended standard amounts. If you have high levels of homocysteine in your blood, you should work with your health practitioner to determine the correct dosages of B-complex supplements.

Fibrinogen is another factor that plays a role in cardiovascular disease. A blood protein, fibrinogen makes blood platelets sticky and is necessary for blood clotting. But, if you have too much fibrinogen in your blood, it becomes sticky and you run the risk of forming blood clots.

Causes of excess fibrinogen include high levels of LDL cholesterol, high blood-sugar levels, obesity, smoking, stress, and synthetic estrogen in birth control pills and hormone replacement therapy. You can keep your fibrinogen levels under control by eating foods, such as garlic and omega-3 fatty acids (found in flaxseeds, salmon, and walnuts), that help keep blood platelets from becoming overly sticky. Regular exercise also helps to keep fibrinogen in a healthy range.

> **Fibrinogen**
> *A blood protein that makes blood platelets sticky and promotes blood clotting. Too much fibrinogen can cause dangerous blood clots.*

A Heart-Healthy Diet

Your diet is a powerful tool in keeping your heart and

circulatory system healthy. Through diet, you can decrease your LDL cholesterol and triglycerides, increase your levels of beneficial HDL cholesterol, and lower your blood pressure. To make the transition to a heart-healthy diet, make sure you are including plenty of fresh fruits and vegetables, fish, green tea, healthy fats (such as olive oil), legumes, nuts, oats, and soy foods in your daily diet. In addition, it is essential to avoid trans-fatty acids completely, limit your intake of refined foods, salt, and sugar, and reduce saturated fats. Here's the rationale behind these suggestions.

Fresh fruits and vegetables are rich sources of antioxidants, which help to prevent free radicals from damaging your heart and arteries, and aid in keeping blood pressure low. Fruits and vegetables are also high in potassium, which is essential for keeping blood pressure in a favorable range. A deficiency of potassium causes cells to retain too much sodium, which increases fluid retention and raises blood pressure. Researchers at the Heart, Lung, and Blood Institute (part of the National Institutes of Health) have developed a diet based on a large-scale research study that identified dietary factors affecting blood pressure. Their recommendations—which have been shown to lower blood pressure as effectively as prescription drugs—emphasize eating eight to ten servings of fruits and vegetables daily.

That's not as daunting as it may seem, when you consider that a serving is one piece of fruit, one-half cup of vegetables, or one cup of leafy greens. A glass of orange juice and blueberries with breakfast, carrot sticks for a snack, a salad, or a bowl of vegetable soup for lunch, a stir-fry with a generous amount of vegetables for dinner, and a fresh fruit bowl for dessert easily meet the goal.

Fresh fruits and vegetables also supply soluble fiber, which helps to sweep excess cholesterol out of the body. Apples, carrots, and citrus fruits are especially good sources, and legumes and some grains (barley and oatmeal) are loaded with this helpful type of fiber. Try to eat between twenty-five and thirty-five grams of fiber daily, with an emphasis on foods rich in soluble fiber.

Fish (especially fish high in omega-3 fatty acids, such as salmon and sardines), raw nuts (such as almonds and walnuts), and healthy fats (such as extra-virgin olive oil) keep arteries flexible, promote the production of beneficial HDL cholesterol, and help to lower blood pressure. Eat at least two servings of omega-3-rich fish weekly, a small handful of nuts, and a tablespoon or more of olive oil daily. Flaxseed oil is also a good source of omega-3 fatty acids and is beneficial for lowering cholesterol. Take one table-spoon daily.

Soy foods, such as soymilk, tempeh, and tofu, have been shown to help lower cholesterol levels. Eat at least one serving of these foods every day. And green tea is a good source of protective antioxidants called polyphenols that help to lower cholesterol and prevent the oxidation of cholesterol. For optimal protection, drink three cups of green tea daily. To prevent bitterness, steep green tea for no more than three minutes. If you are highly sensitive to caffeine, try a decaffeinated variety.

Eliminating certain foods from your diet is also critical for your cardiovascular health. Saturated fats (the most concentrated sources are full-fat dairy products and red meat) and trans-fats (found in partially hydrogenated oils) increase cholesterol levels. In addition, trans-fats raise LDL cholesterol and decrease beneficial HDL cholesterol. It's also best to avoid polyunsaturated oils, such as corn, safflower, and soy oil. When these oils are heated or exposed to light, they quickly become rancid and form compounds that are damaging to the arteries.

In recent years, sugar has been identified as a prime suspect in the development of cardiovascular disease. Eating excessive amounts of sugary foods and refined carbohydrates triggers the production of insulin, a hormone that is secreted by the pancreas and regulates how your cells use sugar. If your cells are subjected to frequent overdoses of sugar and simple carbohydrates, they can lose their ability to respond appropriately to insulin. The result is that the pancreas continues to produce insulin, and elevated levels of insulin raise cholesterol and triglyceride levels and increase blood pressure. To prevent insulin resistance, avoid sugars (which can be disguised as concentrated fruit juice sweeteners, corn syrup, fructose, glucose, honey, lactose, maltose, maple syrup, and sucrose) and refined carbohydrates.

Because sodium may be a factor in hypertension, it's important to cut back on excess salt. Too much sodium can cause water retention, which swells blood volume and increases blood pressure. Reducing your sodium intake is simple if you avoid processed foods, which generally contain large amounts of salt or related sodium compounds, such as monosodium glutamate. In addition, avoid obvious sources of excess sodium, such as chips and salted pretzels. When cooking, you can usually cut in half the amount of salt called for in recipes, and you won't even notice the difference.

Supplements for Cardiovascular Health

A variety of supplements, including herbs, can help keep your heart and cardiovascular system healthy. Antioxidants, such as beta-carotene and other carotenoids, grapeseed extract, selenium, vitamin C, and vitamin E, all help to prevent artery damage caused by free radicals. Grapeseed extract is a rich source of natural compounds, called proanthocyanidins, which have powerful antioxidant properties. These compounds improve circulation, inhibit the oxidation of LDL cholesterol, prevent the clumping of blood platelets that can lead to clots, prevent damage to the arteries, and strengthen the blood vessel walls. Take 50 mg daily as a preventive dose, or 150 mg daily if you have high cholesterol or heart disease.

> **Proanthocyanidins**
> *Natural compounds, found abundantly in grapeseed extract, that have powerful antioxidant properties and help protect the cardiovascular system.*

Coenzyme Q_{10} is one of the most important supplements you can take to protect your cardiovascular system. It is an enzyme that is vital for the production of energy within the cells, and it is found in especially high concentrations in the heart. CoQ_{10} has antioxidant activity, helps to prevent LDL cholesterol from oxidizing, and improves heart function. As a protective dose, take 30–60 mg of CoQ_{10} once a day. If you have cardiovascular disease, take up to 240 mg daily, divided into two equal doses. For best absorption, take CoQ_{10} in gel capsules with a meal that contains some fat.

The B-complex vitamins (especially folic acid, B_6, and B_{12}) help to prevent dangerous levels of homocysteine from accumulating. For most women, taking a B-complex supplement that provides 400 mcg of folic acid, 50 mg of B_6, and 400 mcg of B_{12} will control homocysteine levels. But if you have high levels of homocysteine, you may need larger amounts of these B-vitamins. Consult your healthcare practitioner to determine the appropriate dosage.

Magnesium works in a variety of ways to improve

cardiovascular health. It dilates the coronary arteries, which improves blood flow to the heart, increases beneficial HDL cholesterol, prevents blood platelets from clumping together, and stabilizes heart rhythm. Take 400–600 mg of magnesium daily.

If you are postmenopausal, you shouldn't be eating iron-fortified foods or taking multivitamin supplements that contain iron. Iron can accumulate in your body, promoting free radicals that oxidize cholesterol and damage arteries.

Niacin Therapy for High Cholesterol

Niacin (vitamin B_3) has been recognized for more than fifty years as an effective treatment for lowering cholesterol levels. Not only does niacin decrease total cholesterol, but it also lowers triglycerides and fibrinogen levels, and at the same time increases the levels of beneficial HDL cholesterol. In a 1994 clinical study published in the *Annals of Internal Medicine*, researchers compared niacin and the cholesterol-lowering drug lovastatin. After twenty-six weeks of therapy, patients taking lovastatin had a 32 percent decrease in LDL cholesterol, while those taking niacin had a 23 percent decrease. However, those taking niacin had a 33 percent *increase* in HDL cholesterol, while those taking lovastatin had only a 7 percent increase. Niacin compared reasonably well to drug therapy for decreasing LDL cholesterol, but was clearly the winner for increasing beneficial HDL cholesterol.

Large doses of niacin are necessary for lowering cholesterol, and although the therapy is generally safe, it does cause a harmless flushing of the chest and face. To prevent this reaction, take inositol hexa-niacinate, 500 mg two to three times a day. Do not take sustained-release niacin supplements, because they can be toxic to the liver. If you have diabetes, do not take large amounts of niacin without the supervision of your doctor, because niacin can affect blood-sugar levels.

If you want to use niacin to improve your cholesterol profile, your should have your cholesterol and liver enzymes monitored. Positive results are usually seen in about two months, but may take six months or more, especially for cholesterol levels above 300 mg/dl. When your cholesterol levels go below 200 mg/dl, you can gradually discontinue the niacin and have your cholesterol level checked after two months. If necessary, resume taking niacin until your cholesterol has stabilized at a level below 200 mg/dl.

Herbs for Your Heart

Herbs play a valuable role in a holistic approach to cardiovascular health. Some herbs can be used as tonics to keep your heart and arteries healthy, while others are specific remedies for such problems as high cholesterol and hypertension.

One of the best herbs for your cardiovascular system is one that you probably have in your kitchen.

Garlic (*Allium sativum*) is not only a delicious addition to meals, but has significant effects on cholesterol profiles and blood pressure. When taken regularly, garlic increases beneficial HDL cholesterol, lowers blood pressure, lowers LDL cholesterol and triglycerides, prevents the oxidation of cholesterol that causes artery damage, and reduces the risk of blood clots. Both raw and cooked garlic are beneficial, but raw garlic has more powerful properties. To reap the beneficial effects of garlic, consume one or two cloves per day. If you can't tolerate fresh garlic, take a standardized extract that provides a daily dose of at least 10 mg of alliin (recognized as the active ingredient), which is equal to approximately one clove of fresh garlic.

Hawthorn (*Crataegus oxycantha*) has been used in Europe for centuries as a cardiovascular tonic.

Flavonoids
Powerful antioxidant compounds that help protect cells from free-radical damage.

Hawthorn contains flavonoids (antioxidant compounds) that increase blood flow to the heart, reduce blood pressure, and strengthen and steady the heartbeat. Hawthorn also helps to lower blood pressure, and protects the arteries against free radical damage.

As a protective tonic, hawthorn can be made into a pleasant-tasting tea by pouring one cup of boiling water over two teaspoons of the berries and steeping them for fifteen minutes. Drink two cups daily. If you have cardiovascular disease, take one teaspoon of liquid extract or 120–240 mg of a standardized extract three times daily. The best results are obtained with long-term use. However, if you are taking medication for any type of cardiovascular disease, check with your healthcare professional before taking hawthorn, because it can magnify the effects of cardiovascular drugs.

Guggulipid (*Commiphora mukul*) is an Ayurvedic herb that is used in the treatment of high cholesterol and atherosclerosis. It improves the ability of the liver to process cholesterol, and helps to lower LDL cholesterol while increasing beneficial HDL cholesterol. In clinical studies, guggulipid has been shown to be as effective as pharmaceutical drugs for lowering cholesterol. Guggulipid is generally standardized to contain 2.5 percent guggulsterones. Take 25 mg of guggulsterones three times a day for at least four weeks. Guggulipid is safe, but should not be used during pregnancy because it may stimulate uterine bleeding.

The Importance of Lifestyle

While an appropriate diet and supplements can go a long way toward protecting your cardiovascular system, there's no doubt that other lifestyle factors also play a prominent role in the health of your heart and arteries. Regular exercise, managing stress, and avoiding exposure to toxins are also critical for optimal cardiovascular health.

Your heart is a muscle and needs the stimulus of regular aerobic exercise to be strong and healthy. Exercise also improves circulation, keeps blood pressure low, helps to decrease cholesterol and triglycerides while increasing HDL cholesterol, and is a great stress-reliever. Plan for at least thirty minutes of aerobic exercise five days a week.

Emotional stress can wreak havoc on your heart and cardiovascular system, and addressing the stressors in your life is essential for preventing cardiovascular disease. When you are stressed, adrenaline and other hormones that increase blood pressure and heart rate are released into your bloodstream. Chronic or prolonged stress causes elevated cholesterol, free-radical damage, and high blood pressure. Learning to manage stress is one of the most helpful things you can do to protect your heart and arteries. Deep breathing exercises, meditation, and yoga are all proven ways of reducing stress. For best results, choose a technique of stress management that appeals to you and practice it daily.

Reducing your exposure to environmental toxins is another important factor in preventing cardiovascular disease. Household and garden chemicals, over-the-counter and prescription drugs, and tobacco smoke are all toxins that trigger the production of free radicals that damage arteries. You can decrease your exposure to environmental toxins by avoiding tobacco smoke, buying organic foods, drinking filtered water, using herbs and natural remedies instead of pharmaceutical drugs, and using natural household and garden products.

Supplements for Cardiovascular Health

- B-complex: 50–100 mg daily, containing at least:
  - B_6: 50 mg
  - B_{12}: 400 mcg
  - Folic acid: 400 mcg
- Beta-carotene with mixed carotenoids: 25,000 IU daily
- Vitamin C: 500 mg daily
- Vitamin E: 400 IU daily
- Selenium: 200 mcg daily
- Magnesium: 400–600 mg daily
- CoQ_{10}: 30–60 mg daily (up to 240 mg if you have cardiovascular disease)
- Grapeseed extract: 50–150 mg daily
- Flaxseed oil: 1 tablespoon daily
- Garlic: 1 clove, or 10 mg alliin daily
- Hawthorn: 2 cups tea daily (1 teaspoon fluid extract or 120–240 mg standardized extract three times daily if you have cardiovascular disease)
- Guggulipid: 25 mg gugglesterones (if you have high cholesterol)

CHAPTER 7

How to Buy and Use Nutritional Supplements

It seems that new research appears almost daily regarding the benefits of dietary nutrients, supplements, and herbs and their role in maintaining health. There's no question that dietary supplements make an important contribution to optimal well-being. But choosing between the vast array of products available can be confusing. In reading this book, you've learned about the supplements that are best suited to your particular needs. Now, you need information that will enable you to buy and use supplements with confidence.

Determining Your Supplement Needs

First, it's important to address the question of whether you need to take supplements at all. Unless you live in a pristine environment, eat a perfectly balanced organic diet, get just the right amount of exercise and rest, and are under no stress, then the answer is yes—supplements are a good idea. We live in a world that has a greater number of chemical toxins than ever before in history, and the quality of our air, soil, and water has been seriously compromised. In general, the nutrient content of most foods is diminished because we're not getting food fresh from the garden—instead, it's transported across the country, and sometimes across the world, losing nutrients in the process.

Most of us don't consume even the meager five servings a day of fruits and vegetables recommended by the government for preventing disease. That's far below the recommendations of experts who suggest that, for optimal health, we should be eating approximately nine to ten servings of fruits and vegetables daily. While it's essential to plan for a healthy diet, the reality is that most of us fall short, at least some of the time. This is where dietary supplements can insure that you're providing your body with the nutrients it needs to function optimally and stay healthy.

A good foundation for a supplement program is a well-rounded high-potency multivitamin and mineral. A well-balanced multiple will provide most of the basic nutrients you need. You can then fill in any gaps with additional supplements, and add specific herbs and nutrients that fit your particular needs. It's important, however, to realize that supplements are not a substitute for a healthful diet and lifestyle. No amount of supplements can make up for insufficient sleep, a lack of exercise, a poor diet, or such habits as cigarette smoking or excessive alcohol intake. But by following the dietary and lifestyle suggestions in this book, and taking the recommended supplements, you can be assured that you are taking the right steps to provide your body with all that it needs for optimal health and well-being.

Because people vary somewhat in their nutritional needs, it's necessary to realize that the guidelines this book, or anywhere else, are merely guidelines. The recommendations here are based on the latest research and are safe when taken in the suggested dosages. But you may have greater or lesser needs for certain nutrients, depending on your age, your biochemistry, your genetic heritage, your diet and lifestyle, and your current state of health. To determine what is optimal for you, it's best to work with a health practitioner who is skilled in prescribing dietary supplements.

How to Take Supplements

Taking supplements properly involves more than just gulping them down with a glass of water. Most supplements are assimilated best when taken with, or just after, a meal. This is especially true for supplements that are better absorbed with a meal containing some fat, such as vitamins A, D, E, and CoQ_{10}. A bit of protein also aids in the absorption of minerals. And taking supplements with meals helps prevent the digestive upset that can occasionally occur if you take supplements on an empty stomach. If you are taking liquid herbal supplements, however, they seem to be best absorbed on an empty stomach. Take them a few minutes before a meal, and dilute the dosage with a small amount of water or juice to make them more palatable.

If you can remember to do so, it's also best to divide up supplement dosages so that you're taking them two or three times a day instead of all at once. This provides your body with a consistent supply of nutrients throughout the day, improves absorption, and minimizes the amount that is excreted. For example, with some nutrients, such as calcium, your body can't absorb more than about 500 mg at a time.

Don't err on the side of thinking that more is better. That's not necessarily true, and in the case of certain nutrients, such as vitamins A or D, taking too much can actually be harmful. Even in the case of antioxidants, which are invaluable for protecting cells against damage, taking too much of them can be counterproductive and cause fatigue. Stick with the amounts recommended in this book, or consult your health practitioner if you think you would benefit from larger dosages of any of the supplements recommended here.

Some supplements, such as herbal products, tend to vary greatly in potency. If you're uncertain about how much you should take, it's safe to follow the manufacturer's recommendations on the label. It's also wise to continue educating yourself about your health. There are many excellent books that can guide you in making appropriate choices, including those listed in the References section of this book.

Buying and Storing Supplements

Shelves of natural foods stores, supermarkets, and drug stores are typically stocked with hundreds of nutritional and herbal supplements. If you go into the store knowing what you're looking for, you're ahead of the game. You shouldn't depend on a store clerk to provide you with supplement prescriptions. Although some may be well-educated in the use of supplements, it's best if you have some understanding about which supplements are appropriate for your needs and goals. There are many wonderful resources available, written by leading health experts who can guide you in the right direction. When in doubt, you should consult your healthcare practitioner for advice.

When choosing between various brands of supplements, you'll invariably see a wide variation in price. More expensive is not necessarily better, but just as with most other things in life, there is usually a correlation between price and quality. In other words, you generally get what you pay for. Higher quality products are usually made without artificial colors, preservatives, or sugar.

As far as the question of natural versus synthetic, in

most cases, it doesn't really make a difference. Most nutrients have to go through a significant amount of processing to condense them into a capsule or tablet. But one nutrient that should always be taken in the natural form is vitamin E because the synthetic form is not effective. Natural vitamin E is identified as d-alpha tocopherol (preferably formulated with mixed tocopherols) and synthetic vitamin E is listed on labels as dl-alpha tocopherol.

It's also important to buy supplements in a form that appeals to you. Some people have trouble swallowing large vitamin tablets. Hard tablets can also be difficult to digest, and your body may not break them down efficiently. Capsules of powdered supplements or softgel capsules are usually easier to digest.

To maintain potency, store your supplements in a cool, dark place, such as a kitchen cabinet away from the stove. Don't keep them in the bathroom because high levels of humidity also affect potency. Most supplements should not be refrigerated, either, with the exception of gel capsules of oil-based supplements, such as vitamin E, CoQ_{10}, and evening primrose oil.

To reap the maximum benefits from nutritional supplements, you need to take them consistently. Obviously, if the supplements are just sitting in your kitchen cabinet, they're not doing you any good! To help remember to take your supplements, establish a specific time (for example, always take them immediately after meals). It usually takes a month or two to obtain the benefits of nutritional supplements, and for many herbs, it can take three months or more.

It's important to give dietary supplements time to have an effect. But it's equally important to periodically review the supplements you are taking to make sure they are meeting your needs. At least every six months, inventory the supplements you are taking and review your reasons for taking them. You can then update your supplement program, eliminating those which are no longer a necessity, and adding those that are in line with your current needs.

CONCLUSION

You now have a good understanding of the special health needs you have as a woman, and the role that hormones play in your well-being. From the teenage years through the postmenopausal years, hormones have a significant effect on your emotional and physical health.

As you've discovered, your diet and lifestyle have a great deal to do with how smoothly your hormones perform. A diet that contains excessive alcohol, caffeine, or sugar, and unhealthful fats throws your body off-balance. Equally important to your well-being is your ability to manage stress, how much you exercise, and whether or not you get sufficient sleep and rest.

There's no question that how you live on a daily basis determines the state of your health now and in the years to come. New research emerges almost daily that links diet, exercise, and lifestyle to disease-prevention and longevity. This book contains the most up-to-date information to help you achieve optimal health. At the most basic level, adequate sleep, a nutritious diet, regular exercise, and stress-management skills are the foundation of health. In addition, the supplements recommended in this book provide you with the assurance that you are doing everything possible to provide your body with all that it needs for health, healing, and the prevention of disease.

In reading this book, you've taken an important step toward improving your health and well-being. Be patient with yourself as you make changes in your diet and lifestyle. Small, consistent steps are generally the most successful way to integrate new behaviors. As you begin to feel the positive benefits of caring for yourself in new ways, you'll find subsequent changes easier to make.

I wish you good health in your journey.

SELECTED REFERENCES

Colston, KW, Hansen, CM. Mechanisms implicated in the growth regulatory effects of vitamin D in breast cancer. *Endocrine-Related Cancer*, 2002; (1):45–59.

Feskanich, D, Willett, WC, Stampfer, MJ, Colditz, GA. Milk, dietary calcium, and bone fractures in women: a 12-year prospective study. *American Journal of Public Health*, 1997; 87(6):992–997.

Fischer-Rasmussen, W, Kjaer, SK, Dahl, C, et al. Ginger treatment of hyperemesis gravidarum. *European Journal of Obstetrics & Gynecology, and Reproductive Biology*, 1990; 38:19–24.

Gallo, M, Sarkar, M, Au, W, Pietrzak, K, et al. Pregnancy outcome following gestational exposure to echinacea: a prospective controlled study. *Archives of Internal Medicine*, 2000; 160(20):3141–3143.

Jacobson, TA. Combination lipid-altering therapy: an emerging treatment paradigm for the 21st century.

Current Atheroscleroscierosis Report, 2001; 3(5): 373–382.

Kwasniewska, A, Tukendorf, A, Semczuk, M. Folate deficiency and cervical intraepithelial neoplasia. *European Journal of Gynaecological Oncology,* 1997; 18(6): 526–530.

Maillard, V, Bougnoux, P, Ferrari, P, et al. N-3 and N-6 fatty acids in breast adipose tissue and relative risk of breast cancer in a case-control study in Tours, France. *International Journal of Cancer,* 2002; (1):78–83.

Palan, PR, Mikhail, MS, Romney, SL. Placental and serum levels of carotenoids in preeclampsia. *Obstetrics and Gynecology,* 2001; 98(3):459–462.

Peters-Welte, C, Diessen, M, Albrecht, K. Menstrual abnormalities and PMS: *Vitex agnus-castus* in a study of application. *Gynakologie,* 1994; 7:49–52.

Stevinson, C, Ernst, E. A pilot study of Hypericum perforatum for the treatment of premenstrual syndrome. *British Journal of Obstetrics & Gynaecology,* 2000; 107:870–876.

Stolze, H. An alternative to treat menopausal complaints. *Gynakologie,* 1982; 3(1):14–16.

Thys-Jacobs, S. Micronutrients and the premenstrual syndrome: the case for calcium. *Journal of the American College of Nutrition,* 2000; 19(2): 220–227.

Zhang, S, Hunter, DJ, Forman, MR, et.al. Dietary carotenoids and vitamins A, C, and E and risk of breast cancer. *Journal of the National Cancer Institute*, 1999; 91(6):547–556.

OTHER BOOKS AND RESOURCES

Murray, M, and Pizzorno, J. *Encyclopedia of Natural Medicine, revised second edition.* Rocklin, CA: Prima Publishing, 1998.

Northrup, C. *Women's Bodies, Women's Wisdom.* New York, NY: Bantam Books, 1998.

Vukovic, L. *Herbal Healing Secrets for Women.* Paramus, NJ: Prentice Hall, 2000.

Vukovic, L. *14-Day Herbal Cleansing.* Paramus, NJ: Prentice Hall, 1998.

GreatLife Magazine
Consumer magazine with articles on vitamins, minerals, herbs, and foods.
Available for free at many health and natural food stores.

Let's Live Magazine

Consumer magazine with emphasis on the health benefits of vitamins, minerals, and herbs.

Customer service:

1-800-676-4333

P.O. Box 74908

Los Angeles, CA 90004

Subscriptions: 12 issues per year, $19.95 in the U.S.; $31.95 outside the U.S.

Physical Magazine

Magazine oriented to body builders and other serious athletes.

Customer service:

1-800-676-4333

P.O. Box 74908

Los Angeles, CA 90004

Subscriptions: 12 issues per year, $19.95 in the U.S.; $31.95 outside the U.S.

The Nutrition Reporter™ newsletter

Monthly newsletter that summarizes recent medical research on vitamins, minerals, and herbs.

Customer service:

P.O. Box 30246

Tucson, AZ 85751-0246

e-mail: jack@thenutritionreporter.com

www.nutritionreporter.com

Subscriptions: $26 per year (12 issues) in the U.S.; $32 U.S. or $48 CNC for Canada; $38 for other countries

National Women's Health Information Center
1-800-994-WOMAN (1-800-994-9662)
Website: www.4woman.gov

The American College of Obstetricians and Gynecologists
1-202-863-2518
Website: www.acog.org

INDEX